Ride On

IN SONG AND STORY

Ride On

IN SONG AND STORY

JIMMY MacCARTHY

TOWN
HOUSE
DUBLIN

Hardback edition published in 2002
This edition published in 2006 by
TownHouse, Dublin
THCH Ltd
Mount Pleasant Business Centre
Mount Pleasant Avenue
Ranelagh
Dublin 6

1   2   3   4   5   6   7   8   9   10

A CIP catalogue record for this book is available from the British Library.

ISBN 1-86059-265-1
978-186059-265-2

Cover and text design by Anú Design, Tara
Typeset by Anú Design
Printed by WS Bookwell, Finland

Contents

8

For my parents Ted & Betty

with love

Acknowledgements

Over the years, I have received a great deal of help from my family, friends and fellow musicians. Some of them have been mentioned in this book already, but some others I want to salute here.

I wrote 'Diamond Days' in the Carmel Hotel in Kilkenny. It was always a pleasure to play in the Carmel and many thanks to Greg Flannery for all his support and hospitality over the years.

The Committee of the Cork Folk Festival have always been generous in their promotion of me and have given me headlining status as early as they possibly could, and repeatedly so, for which my thanks to Jimmy Walsh, Hammy Hammond and the Committee as a whole for the leg up.

I would like to salute my Swiss friend, the musician and producer Martin Fischer, aka Chicken. Life with Chicken was a roller-coaster ride and a lot of fun and I'm glad to have known his particular brand of magic.

My first attempt to record a single was 'Strain Of The Dance' which was produced by Donal Lunny and, for that, all praise would only be stating the obvious. I have only worked with Donal on one other occasion, co-writing a song for the sound track of the Turkish film *Tears*. Giving me that job I saw as an act of generosity on his part.

Sincere thanks to The Yeats Society for allowing me to use Jack Yeats' master-piece, *The Singing Horseman*, on the cover of my album of the same name.

I would like to say a special thanks to my sister Stacey for her support with regard to my career and business affairs in general over the years and in particular for her help on my *Dreamer* album.

My thanks to the legendary Louis Walsh for suggesting that I send a copy of my compilation album *Warmer for the Spark* to the major publishing companies and for his introductions to the people concerned.

My thanks to Treasa Coady of TownHouse for giving me this opportunity. My sincerest thanks to Marie Heaney and Claire Rourke for their painstaking work in giving me a book that I already love.

12

A very special thank you to Hugh Duffy · All the Ryans (Rath Beag) · All the MacCarthy Clan (Silvergrove) · My Aunt Maire Thompson · My Uncle Seamus Manley · My Uncle Sean MacCarthy and family · All the Wall family · Marilyn, Pat and Bobby Buckley · Richard (Titch) and Angie Walsh · Aidan Bowles · Barbara Bowles · Olive Bowles · Mick McGrath · Paddy McClintock · Shay Healy · Greg Boland · Andrew Boland · Owen O'Neill · Hal O'Neill · Mick Crowley (Crowley's Music Shop, Cork) · Ken and Ger Kiernan · Siobhan Lynham · Ciaran and Lynda Brennan · Jim McAllister · Her excellency Mary McAleese · Matthew Gilsenan, Niall Morris and James Nelson (The Celtic Tenors) · Shay and Mark (The Folk House) · Eadeen,

Imelda and Marie (The Energy Givers) · Pat Egan · Caroline, Layla and David · Elaine Tiernan · Ann, Mazie and Mary · Fidelma Allen · Sarah Allen · Brian Kennedy · Sinead O'Connor · Peter O'Mahony · Mandy Murphy and all of the Murphy Family · Lynn Kavanagh and family · Eve Hughes · Susan and Ivor Fitzpatrick · Michael Murphy and Angela Kelly · Agnes Jameson · All at Curraheen Drive · Maura, Mac and Jessy Bennett · Pat Longley · Geoff Walsh (Fairlands Vet) · Rachel Bennett · Theo Dorgan · Paula Meehan · Micheal Sheridan · Declan and Rowena Young · Derek Nelson (Guitar Maker and Doctor) · Patrick Bergin · Liam O'Muirthile · Finbarr and all of the Hurley Family · Kieran Goss · Joe and Luan Parle · Mick Daly (Good Teacher) · Tana O'Brien · Fran Bergin · All the Raggy Ball Rovers · David and Adele Agnew · David Downs · Maureen O'Donnell · Simon O'Mahony · Joan Hastings · Graham Lyle · Honor Heffernan · The Corrs · Louis Walsh · Mike MacCormack, Jamie Campbell, Willie Morrison and Lizzie Hurst (Universal Publishing) · Jan and Chris McDermott · Torsten and Niels Kinsella (Super AD) · Tommy and Karin Kinsella · All at IMRO · All at MCPS · Victor Finn · Adrian Gaffney · Charlie O'Neill · Kieran Q Egan · Jerry McDonald · Noel and Mary Shine · Sinead Lohan and all her family · Mrs Murphy · Myriam Kavanagh · Paul and Natalie · Danny Kenny (The Westwood) · Ted, Bridie and all the Jones Family · Mike Scott (The Waterboys) · Fiona and John Prine · Eleanor Shanley · Maureen Kelly · Ashford House · Leo O'Kelly · Nicky Moment and her Dad · Sonny Condell · Tommy Jordan · Frank and Rita Kennedy (The Alexander Technique) · Tom Wilson (Voice Coach) · David Fitzgerald · Bim O'Sullivan · David Coleman · Jean, Susan and Allen Crosbie · Helen Kieley · Deirdre Lehane · Mick and Carol Begley · Joe O'Callaghan · Sir George Martin · Carol Conboy · Mr and Mrs Dunlea · Ray and Dick Dunlea · Ed Christman (*Billboard* magazine) ·

13

All at *Irish Music Magazine* · All at *Hot Press* · Rebecca Storm · Sandy Kelly · Linda Martin · Elvis Presley · The Beatles · Pete Brennan and John Madden (The Garage Band) · Brian Calnan (Drummer, Percussion) · Christy O'Connell · Ivan O'Shea · Ita Malony · Finbar and all The Fureys · Charlie McGettigan (The Baggot Inn) · Charlie McGettigan (Songwriter) · Paul Harrington · Lesley Dowdall · John Lapin (Thank you to 'Evolving Music' with Sony and UMP UK) · Rob Burke · Scott Gunter · Pat Alger · Kent Blazey · Dave Prim · John Dillon (Irish Voice) · Kathrine Kerby · Daire Winston · Paul Ash Brown · John Gibson · The artist Rasher · David Hull (Promotions) · Denis O'Reilly · Ruth Elliott · Frankie and Tracy Gavin · Tommy Fleming · Mairead O'Reilly · Dan Dan Fitzgerald · Johnny Fang Murphy (Stargazer) · Chris Ahern · Sheila Cassidy and family · John O'Shea (Killarney) · Sky MacCarthy · Sean Keane · Dolores Keane · John Faulkner · Neil Toner · Finbarr Wright · Ronan Tynan · Bernice Corcoran · Patsy Denehy · Martha Healy · Hansey Kelleher · Alice and Johnny Ruth · Micheal and Mary Moran · Matt Cranich (Sliabh Notes) · Tommy O'Sullivan (Sliabh Notes) · Cindy Riech · Stuart Smith · Tijum Tutty · Benny Rice · Leo Barnes · Liam O'Maonlaí · Francis McPadden · Jerry Fealey · Thomas and Mrs Byrne · Shay and Marion Dunne · Sean McGuire · Wanda, Shaney and Christine (The Pogues) · Tim Martin · Seamus O'Neill · Phillip Bodger · Teresa and all the Riney Family · Anne Dunne (The Briery Gap) · Paul Wade (Piano Tuner) · Rodney Crowl · The stunningly brilliant Conor Reeves · Thom Nicholls · Tim Laws · Danny Osbourne (Artist) · David Hanly · Patrick Collins · Niel Prenderville (Cork's 96FM) · Donna O'Sullivan · John Creedon · Tony Burke, Tara and Finbar (Dixies) · All in the village of Rathnew · Bobby Moriarty · The Whistlers · The Bubbles · Seamus Begley · Ger Coffey · Laiose MacReamoinn · Noreen Strong · Rob and Andrew Strong · Lynne Earls ·

Billy Robinson · John Cook · Russ Ballard · Mark Kennedy · Sammy Nevin · Derek Fey · Jerry Crowe (Perfect Pitch) · Veronique and Niall O'Leary · Dick Farley · Kian Egan (Westlife) · Joe Herlihy · Jack L · Neil Walton (Walton's Music) · Eamon Murray (Soul on Air) · Rina O'Grady · Antony Bebawi and Niel Adelman (Harbottle and Lewis) · Jimmy Smith · Jenny Newman · Brendan Graham · Ger MacCarthy (London) · Freddy and Anne White · Gayle and Tony Davis · Jim Kennedy · Helen and Cimile Strong · Philip Begley · Paddy Woodworth (*The Irish Times*) · Joe Jackson · Declan Lynch · Paul Dromey · Tony Clayton-Lea · Nancy Iverson · Micheal D Higgins · Madaline Sieler · Donagh Long · Joe and Roxanne Fritsch · Peter Sheridan · Anto Drennan · Paul Moore · Des Moore · Tommy Moore · Mick and Delia Cunningham · Tom and Deirdre Costelloe · Brian Malloy · Noel V Ginnity · Byril and Ian McKenzie · Ann O'Sullivan · Ola and Maria Ballack · Kevin Finnerty · John and Clare Barry

15

Introduction

Writing this book has been a labour of love. I have written it in my own way, in my own words. But I must say that without the invaluable advice of my old friends, the poets Theo Dorgan and Paula Meehan, also the writer Michael Sheridan, it could easily have gone astray. Having started out on this journey, I had planned to write a pen-picture backdrop to how these fifty-three songs came about, but without betraying the muse. I soon found that there was no separating the songs from my life's path and that to offer a view of the work, one needed at least a glimpse of the life. So, with the omission of my earliest years with my grandfather James Manley in Mill Street, County Cork, and my time at the Presentation Brothers' College and the Christian Brothers' College, this book becomes a reasonable, if feint, line drawing of my life to date.

1

Ancient Rain

Ancient Rain

The summer joy is surely gone
When every clock the hour had on
Last night we masqued and merry made
Under the full moon madness played
An older witch, she danced with me
And later sat upon my knee
A fiddler flashed his fiddler's grin
To hell and back from lock to chin

The witch was clean pushed off my knee
By one born one day after me
And we went home with lock and key
She left me in the morning

I slept on till one o'clock
And walked out like a concrete block
I drank some whiskey and I drank it hot
On the first day of winter

Chorus *Ancient rain, pouring down*
Wire my bones to the ground
Ancient rain, pouring down
Wire my bones to the ground

The summer joy is surely gone
When every clock the hour had on
Last night we massed and merry made
Under the full moon madness played
While these demons taunt in pagan time
Past and present now in rhyme
Two hands that squeeze my life away
On this the holy All Saints' Day

Chorus *Ancient rain, pouring down*
Wire my bones to the ground
Ancient rain, pouring down
Wire my bones to the ground

'Ancient Rain' sets the scene for a masqued, exotic and frenzied Hallowe'en gathering from the perspective of the morning after with regard to the night before. It was a fancy-dress Hallowe'en céilí in Connolly Hall in Cork in the early 1980s that inspired this song. The event was organised by Timmy MacCarthy, aka 'Timmy the Brit', the man who almost single-handedly revived the set-dancing tradition. On that same night, if my memory serves me well, he played button accordion with the Surreal Céilí Orchestra while, on fiddle, there was the fine player Seamus Creagh.

People came as demons, ghouls, fairies, witches, Cú Chulainn, the Pope, Joe Dolan – I went as myself. Our pagan bones danced till the early hours. The following morning, I woke with a hangover that screamed for a hair of the dog, so I made my way to the Long Valley for a hot whiskey or two. Someone mentioned that it was All Saints' Day and I thought of the night before; of our pagan bones, holy places, of our Christian feast and painted faces, and of the ancient rain.

23

2

The Mad Lady and Me

The Mad Lady and Me

Among the walls and ruins
And the horrid cynic stone
I walk without a lover
For my older bones
The sun was strong
In going down
It was a dreamlike day
'Twas there I met the trinity
And there I heard them say:

Chorus Bye bye mama, bye brother John
Fare thee well you Shandon Bells
Ring on, ring on

She leaned and leaned much closer
And hugged them all goodbye
Her mother cried, 'Don't go my love
We all must by and by.'
A drunken tongue said
'Leave her off she'll drive us all crazy.'
She turned around and saw my face
And both of us were she

Chorus And we sang
Bye bye mama, bye brother John
Fare thee well you Shandon Bells
Ring on, ring on

Up on to the limestone wall
And down the ladder steps
She threw herself into the stream
With a splash of no regrets
Side-stroke swimming midstream
Throwing kisses to the crowd
And everything was silent
And the sky had not one cloud

Chorus   *But for*

> *Bye bye mama, bye brother John*
> *Fare thee well you Shandon Bells*
> *Ring on, ring on*
> *We were swimming out on the sunset*
> *We were swimming out to sea*
> *Swimming down past the Opera House*
> *The mad lady and me, and we sang,*
> *'Bye bye mama, bye brother John*
> *Fare thee well you Shandon Bells*
> *Ring on, ring on, ring on.'*

It was the perfect summer's day when I walked out on Camden Quay. I followed the limestone wall of the river on to Pope's Quay, and there, in front of St Mary's Church (a magnificent limestone façade with monumental pillars and thirty-foot high red doors, giving the appearance more of a temple of Isis rather than a Roman Catholic church), stood a most unlikely trinity. A little Cork lady wearing a mac and a headscarf, on what might have been the hottest day of the year. Her son, who they called John, seemed to be a right bit of work and drunken abuse ran from his mouth. Her daughter, the Mad Lady, was a tall, thin girl with long, black hair, pale and wan. (As they'd say in Cork, 'Isn't your wan very wan?' Mind you, there's a pub up in Barrack Street called The Three Wans but that's just because it's 111 Barrack Street.) Anyway, the girl was hugging and kissing her mother goodbye, saying, 'I'm off now, Mama.' Her mother cried, 'Don't go, my love, you'll break my heart!' The son then joined in the escalating cacophony with a drunken roar, 'Leave her off! She'll drive us all crazy.' With that she took herself to the water's edge and threw herself into the Lee, swimming side-stroke out into the stream and down past the Opera House. By now, the fire brigade had arrived in their yellow jackets, they rescued and returned the Mad Lady to the establishment she had checked out of a little earlier on that same day – known to all as the 'Lee Road Hilton'. Everything bar the jacuzzi, I believe. I've never stayed there myself, but it has been recommended.

3

Ride On

Ride On

True you ride the finest horse
I have ever seen
Standing sixteen-one or two
With eyes wild and green
And you ride the horse so well
Hands light to the touch
And I could never go with you
No matter how I wanted to

Chorus *Ride on, see ya*
I could never go with you
No matter how I wanted to

And when you ride into the night
Without a trace behind
Run the claw along my gut
One last time
I'll turn to face an empty space
Where you used to lie
And smile for the spark that
Lights the night
Through a teardrop in my eye

Chorus   *Ride on, see ya*
I could never go with you
No matter how I wanted to
No matter how I wanted to

People often ask me about this song but, purely and simply, it is a song of parting. The parting of lovers, the parting of emigrants from their homeland and friends, the parting when illness or accident takes the life of a loved one. I have been asked to sing this song at many funeral services and, somehow, it always feels right.

Christy Moore recorded this song on his *Ride On* album in 1984 and it was my first hit. I will always be grateful to him for giving me the start with what would have been then regarded as a most unlikely song-writing voice.

Christy obviously recognised 'Ride On' as a song of parting when, on its release, he dedicated it to the memory of the great Luke Kelly.

I am often asked about the line 'Run the claw along my gut one last time' (in the same way as I'm asked about the line 'I am the geek with the alchemist's stone', from my song 'The Bright Blue Rose'). These dramatic lines jolt the listener into a deeper engagement, or at least this was my intention in employing such devices. That is not to say that they were not a natural part of the flow of expression but, while most writers would edit them out, I feel that a song, like life, depends on the decisions one makes and these decisions were not taken lightly. Some people may think that I just throw paint at the canvas, but there is exactitude and detail in the placing of every word and phrase until I am satisfied that the lyric is absolutely watertight. It has always bothered me that the previously mentioned line from 'Ride On' has often been changed to 'Run *your* claw along my gut one last time', which clearly denotes an intention to cause pain, when the pain I envisioned is simply the pain of living life. The pain of parting and separation that no life can escape. Life is hard. Ride on.

4

The Contender · That Face

The Contender

When I was young, and I was in my day
Sure I'd steal what woman's heart there was away
And I'd sing into the dawning
Song ablaze into the morning
Long before I was the man you see today
I was born beneath a star that promised all
I could have lived my life between Cork, Cóbh and Youghal
But the wheel of fortune took me
From the highest point, she shook me
By the bottle live, by the bottle I shall fall

Chorus   *There in the mirror on the wall*
        I see the dream is fading
        From the contender to the brawl
        The ring, the rose, the matador raving

        And when I die, I'll die a drunk down on the street
        He will count me out to ten in clear defeat
        Wrap the Starry Plough around me
        Let the piper's air resound me
        And there I'll rest until the Lord of Love I'll meet

Chorus   *There in the mirror on the wall*
        I see the dream is fading
        From the contender to the brawl
        The ring, the rose, the matador raving

        Wrap the Starry Plough around me,
        Let the piper's air resound me
        And there I'll rest until the Lord of Love I'll meet

'The Contender' is a song about a man who had everything and blew it.
Britain had never seen anything like Jack Doyle. In 1933, he drew 90,000
fans to the White City to watch him box. He was earning £600 a week on
stage as a singer, and all of this at the age of nineteen. Born into a poor family

in Cobh in County Cork in 1913, it was Jack Doyle's dream to fight like Jack Dempsey and to sing like John McCormack.

His good looks, charm and athletic figure brought him to Hollywood, where this fine-featured, six-foot-five Adonis socialised with such greats as Clarke Gable and Errol Flynn. He had an affair with the motor-industry heiress Delphine Dodge. The singing playboy's motto was 'a generous man never went to hell' and, by the time he was thirty, he was well on his way to squandering his three-quarters of a million pound fortune.

Later he fell in love with the Mexican singer and movie star, Movita. He married her and they returned to Britain and Ireland where their touring show reaped huge financial rewards. The couple achieved a celebrity status comparable to Burton and Taylor, arguably more attractive but with equal fire in the relationship. But Jack's drinking, carousing and sexual exploits destroyed the marriage. Movita fled to America and Doyle ended up singing for his supper in the bars of London and Dublin, where he spent much of his time in a brothel in the red-light district run by the legendary Madam Dolly Fawcett, who held the fallen idol in great and tender esteem. Movita later married Marlon Brando.

Doyle never really got over the love of his life. He missed Movita desperately as he sank, literally, to gutter level. But throughout his bad times, he maintained an incredible spirit and dignity as he moved through the netherworlds of Dublin and London, where he died penniless on the street in 1978. He was brought back in triumphant fashion to his native Cobh where he was buried with great style and celebration.

I first heard something of the Jack Doyle story from my father who got drunk with the legendary hell-raiser when Jack and 'Iron man' Butty Sugrue, on their way to a demonstration bout at Puck Fair in Killorglan, dropped in to the Terence Hotel bar in Macroom, which belonged to my grandmother Hannah MacCarthy.

She had bought the premises when it was called The Victoria but changed the name to The Terence in memory of the hunger striker Terence MacSweeney.

This was my parents' first home after they married and it was here I was born on 28 January 1953. Some years later, my father discovered Alcoholics Anonymous and adhered to its philosophy for the rest of his life, bar the occasional lost weekend. I returned home to my parents' house at the age of thirty and, with my father's incredible support, I surrendered to the same programme – to hand my life over to God as I understood him to be, and, one day at a time, not to take that first drink. I have been sober now for nineteen years and, though still very far from perfect, I feel I owe my blessed life to this programme. I wonder if Jack Doyle had found his way into any of the countless AA rooms all over the world would his story have been a different one. It was with this recognition of a fellow alcoholic that I wrote 'The Contender' and 'That Face'.

'That Face' is a collection of lyric scraps that were all written in a state of hangover (at which I excelled) and conveniently fell together to make this piece.

That Face

Spirit and bright one
Have you left me for dead?
Once light burned in these eyes
Now they're pale and bled
I see morning with no mystery

And the darkness holds only dread for me
And so it goes when you travel by bottle
Ride the wall of death
Blind on full throttle
And it's a hard place to escape from
And you're a hard case
When you're on your way down

See the blue boy
Under the silver moon
He can't see her
Though she's right there in the room
So he strolls downtown
To the drowning places
Get the whiskey down ya boy
Paint a smile upon the faces
But he's not free tonight

Chorus To look at the love upon that face
To look at the light she throws upon a darkened place
To look at the world that bore her
To look at the hands before her
To look at the love upon that face

So he sings his songs
With his soul on the strings
And he's cutting his throat

With his peacocks and rings
Wild eyed and crazy
Like a raven in the night
So full of lonely and the whiskey bite
I found these words today
Among my masterpieces
Something I scrawled out
For my Masters thesis
As for this hopeless liquid philosophy
I could justify
I just could not see

Chorus To look at the love upon that face
To look at the light she throws upon a darkened place
To look at the world that bore her
To look at the hands before her
To look at the love upon that face

39

5

Don't You Still Smile

Don't You Still Smile

Take yesterday's sorrow
And then from tomorrow
You borrow the hope of a smile
You watch love go under and listen to thunder
And wonder is it worth your while
And don't you still smile
Your tears you must spill
Then but over the hill
And you just can't resist that old ride
It always looks best where
Until you can get there
You're always leaning to the greener side

And don't you still smile
Though you don't look as keen
You're still chasing the dream
You know that it's there
You know that it's there

And yet there's regret
For the time that we let slip away
When we could have done more
You watch love go under
The clap of the thunder
The empty pockets and the bolted doors
And don't you still smile
Though you don't look as keen
You're still chasing the dream
You know that it's there
You know that it's there

Take yesterday's sorrow
And then from tomorrow
You borrow the hope of a smile

Jimmy and his running dogs, a bunch of young kids, came down from Scotland. They had finished school and, there being little prospect of work, made their way to London. Theirs was the punk generation, with all its diverse paraphernalia of safety pins, chains, mohican haircuts and tartan. The symbol of anarchy seemed to be their chosen badge and they were big fans of the band Crass who professed this political doctrine.

When I first met them, they were ten in number but, within a week, that number had more than doubled. They were beautiful-looking people, young and very gentle and they shared everything. I would see them running hell-for-leather down Earl's Court Road with loaves of bread stuffed inside their jackets and the rookies hot on their trail. This was 1979–80 – the beginning of the Thatcher era – when cutbacks and shutdowns were the order of the day. We all lived together in a huge hospital building on its own grounds, just off the Old Brompton Road. The sickly sweet smell of glue hung on the air, ever present everywhere. In fact you could not avoid its effect as these young people walked the long corridors sniffing this economical opium from plastic bags.

This alternative accommodation was known as squatting; it required breaking into an abandoned building, changing the locks and negotiating afterwards with the local housing authority. There were many dangers to life, limb and personal property, particularly from the British Movement, a faction of the National Front, skinheads, neo-Nazi style racists who had punks on their hate list, along with many ethnic groups. They broke in to our squat on one occasion.

I had just arrived from Ireland with Davey White after the demise of our band Southpaw. Southpaw, which is the term used for a left-handed boxer, consisted of Johnny Campbell on bass, Davey White on drums, Teddy Moynihan

43

on guitar and keyboard and, for a spell, Gerry McConnell on piano. In the musical director's chair was the inimitable Declan Sinnott, who earlier had been the other half of a duo with me under our own name. Though this was my first serious band, the others were professionals who had travelled extensively and played with such greats as Gino Washington, Rory Gallagher and Chuck Berry, while Declan had been a member of the first, Irish, super Celtic rock group – Horslips – which he left on grounds of artistic principles, I believe. Even in those early days, he was widely regarded as a consummate and gifted musician.

For me, the highlights of playing with Southpaw were not the performances on stage or in the studio, but when Declan strapped on the Fendar telecaster in a rehearsal room and went to work on the arrangement of a brand-new song. It was like catching a glimpse of a rare, elusive and majestic creature, which induced awe in all of us.

Johnny Campbell was the one that held the band together, and he was tireless in this. When we were at school, my brother Dan and I had a garage band and we used to see Johnny play with a group called the Chymes for school dances. The first time we saw them play, Johnny was on drums and singing the Hollies' number 'Look Through Any Window' and he seemed to us to exude a magical light. His manner and, to a lesser degree, his appearance has always reminded me of my grandfather James Manley.

Later Johnny and I formed another combo – The Jimmy MacCarthy Band – with James Delaney on piano and Paul Moran on drums and we have continued to play in bands together over the years, sometimes seriously, sometimes for fun, but always of value to me. Even though I don't see Johnny very much these days, I still regard him as one of my best friends.

It was during these first early days working with Declan and with him in mind that I penned 'Don't You Still Smile'.

44

6

Miles of Eyes · I Feel Like an Island
Players in the Light

Miles of Eyes

I'm going back
I can't stay here
Miles and miles of lonely eyes
I'm going back
To Mama's arms
Miles of eyes dehumanised
I hear the sound of hungry hearts
Calling to a time gone by

The paling skin of the day
Miles of eyes dehumanised

Chorus   *I'm so bored with the everyday*
I'm so bored with the everyday
I'm so bored with the everyday

I know I've been before I am
Before I lived beneath these lies
Soldiers in the ranks of time
They all lived before they died
I'm going back
I can't stay here
Miles and miles of lonely eyes
I'm going back to Mama's arms
Miles of eyes dehumanised

Chorus   *I'm so bored with the everyday*
I'm so bored with the everyday
I'm so bored with the everyday

47

I Feel Like an Island

You bring home yellow flowers
To brighten up the room
And I lean to the skylight
Like a tunnel from the tomb
And I know it's not the love
Cause the love is like a diamond
Till I see you again
I'm going to feel like an Island

I'm swimming in the streetlights
I'm singing to the stars
Just a fool at the table
Blowing really fine cards
But when the reel rolls at night
It's just the stars and the diamond
And a sorcerer's spell
That makes me feel like an Island

Chorus *I feel like an Island, an Island, an Island*
I feel like an Island, an Island tonight
I feel like an Island, an Island, an Island
I feel like an Island, an Island tonight

Now I bring yellow flowers
To brighten up the room

For forgiveness, for love
For an empty tomb
It's the love of my life
It's a love like a diamond
And never again
To feel like an Island

To get back to the London saga. With regard to slumming it, this was a first for Davey, the drummer from Southpaw and, within a few weeks, he moved on. He left, I think, as a result of the break-in incident with the British Movement, aggravated by a piece of graffiti printed on his room wall that read *'Kill all Irish Catholic Bastards'*.

I stayed on and settled down to some sort of routine. In the mornings, life kicked in quite early, as some of my fellow inmates were working on the building sites. I would head out for breakfast at about ten and return to find Jimmy and his flock of punks preening themselves for a day at Buckingham Palace, where they would pose for a fee for the stream of tourists who came to this magnificent monument to a depleted empire. I would write for a couple of hours before taking the Tube to Leicester Square, where I would busk in the underground until evening and then retire to the Pizza Hut for pizza and coffee. Here I would count my coins and convert them into notes before heading home. Then I would strike out for three or four pints of Ruddle's County Real Ale. After that, I couldn't say for sure what my movements were, but I would find my way home and do the same thing all over again the following day. It was to this backdrop of the paling skin of the day and the hankering back to a more natural time that I wrote 'Miles Of Eyes'.

It was also during this spell in London in 1979–80 that I wrote 'I Feel Like An Island', obviously a song of isolation. I had two verses and a chorus written and, for about twelve years, could go no further till, one day, I found a quotation by the American poet Walt Whitman which said that Christianity was based on forgiveness, love, and an empty tomb, and I said, 'Yes! Verse three. "I Feel Like An Island". Thanks be to God.'

'Players In The Light' is a song that was written in the back of a Ford Transit van on the way to a gig in Clare and was originally titled 'Soldiers Of The Heart', and I think it captures the idealism of the whole Southpaw experience. To this day, I believe that the band had the potential to be a great band. But we toured the country for little more than petrol and food money and borrowed from our manager, Elvera Butler, to make excellent demos that we never sent to anyone. Our gigs were electric and, to a man, we delivered as if every performance was our last.

Players in the Light

Soldiers of the heart
In the shadows of the road
Like men on a mission
With a timeless code
Leaning to the headlights

And the engine's minor drone
Children's eyes and fingers
On bodies tired and grown

Soldiers of the heart
All the players in the light
As they head for home again
Eternal headlights in the night
Pilgrims to the shrine
Of life in obscure rhyme
Still clinging to the heartbeat
Of a live band in time

See the dark figures
Shuffle in the spotlight
Like blind men in the moonlight
Wading fields of morning dreams

Soldiers of the heart

7

Shuffle of the Buckled

Shuffle of the Buckled

The moon was full
And the hearts were empty
When I stopped to watch the river go down
Saw the gleaming eyes
On your blind to corners
Heard the shuffle of the buckled
As they come to lay their money down

Chorus   *Ooh – not even with his money down*
And he fades in the shadows
Of the walls of night in this town
He just fades in the shadows
Of the walls of night in this town

My heart was numb
And my eyes stopped running
And the wind chilled my bones
Where I stood to watch that river go down
And the song of this street
Boasts no chest-proud anthem
It's called the 'Shuffle of the Buckled'
As they come to lay their money down

Chorus   *Ooh – not even with his money down*
And he fades in the shadows
Of the walls of night in this town
He just fades in the shadows
Of the walls of night in this town

Not even with his money down

When I came back to Ireland, Seamus O'Neill of Mulligan Records put out my first single, the previously mentioned 'Miles Of Eyes' and later, in 1981, put out a second single called 'Like In The Movies', produced by the celebrated composer Shawn Davy. On the B-side of 'Miles Of Eyes' was 'Shuffle Of The Buckled', a song written about a walk through Cork's red-light district after closing time one night. It was at the Parnell Place end of Oliver Plunkett Street that I saw a hunched and deformed figure approach a lady of the night. She refused him and, as he shuffled off, I watched him fade into the shadows of the walls of night.

8

Mystic Lipstick · Missing You

A Hard Man to Follow

Mystic Lipstick

She wears mystic lipstick
She wears stones and bones
She tells myth and legend
She sings rock and roll
She wears chains of bondage
She wears wings of hope
She wears the gown of plenty
And still it's hard to cope

Chorus *Croí, ó mo chroí your heart is breaking*
Your eyes are red; your song is blue
Your poets underneath the willow in despair
They have been lovers of your sad tune
Lovers of your slow air

And though they feed on what hurts you
To sing the book of your heart
Oh sweet black rose how they've loved you
And it's hard to
But they do, Éire, they do

She keeps fools for counsel
She keeps wig and gown
The cloth and the bloody warfare
The Stars and Stripes and Crown
Still we pray for a better day now
God willing it's for the best
But I've just see the harp on a penny
With a dollar on her naked breast

57

Chorus *Croí, ó mo chroí your heart is breaking*
Your eyes are red; your song is blue
Your poets underneath the willow in despair
They have been lovers of your sad tune
Lovers of your slow air
Lovers in sweet despair

Missing You

In nineteen hundred and eighty six
Not much work for a chippie or swinging the pick
And you can't live on love, and on love alone
So you sail o'er the ocean, away 'cross the foam

To where you're a Paddy, and where you're a Mick
Not much use at all bar stacking the brick
And your mate was a spade and he carried the hod
Two old heavy horses, heavily shod

Chorus *Oh I'm missing you, I'd give all for*
The price of the flight
Oh I'm missing you, under
Piccadilly's neon

And who did you murder and are you a spy
I'm just fond of the drink, helps me laugh, helps me cry
And I took to the port for a permanent high
Now I laugh a lot less, and I'll cry 'til I die

Now the summer is fine but the winter's a fridge
Wrapped up in old cardboard under Charing Cross Bridge
And I'll never go home, it's because of the shame
Of a misfit's reflection in a shop windowpane

So all you young people take an advice
Before crossing an ocean you'd better think twice
'Cos you can't live without love, without love alone
Here's the proof 'round the West End in the nobody zone

Chorus *Oh I'm missing you, I'd give all for*
The price of the flight
Oh I'm missing you, under
Piccadilly's neon

A Hard Man to Follow

I've been to the moon
With the Queen of the night
Circled the sun
And maintained my sight
I've been to the deep
With the dolphin to play
Beneath the golden bough
With Buddha to pray
And we sang

Chorus   *Fol dol de dee*
Fol dol de day
All through the night
And the following day

I've ridden on the back
Of a magical steed
A dancer reborn
Messiah indeed
And once I did live
In a biblical time
Been to a feast
Seen water turn to wine
And we sang

Chorus   *Fol dol de dee*
Fol dol de day
All through the night
And the following day

Sure I'm a hard man to follow
A hard man to follow
A hard man to follow, me
A hard man to follow
A hard man to follow
A hard man to follow, me

Chorus   *Fol dol de dee*
           Fol dol de day
           All through the night
           And the following day

'Mystic Lipstick' is written in traditional Roisín Dubh style, depicting Ireland as a woman and addressing her plight. From the eight hundred years of oppressive occupation and its legacy, the Northern Question, to the recession, unemployment, and consequent emigration of the 1980s, I simply lay bare the facts.

'Missing You' is a song that highlights the plight of those who left Ireland in search of work in the building trade in the mid-1980s. In my time in England, and especially when I lived in Arlington Road, Camden Town, I heard many stories of those who came to make big money, hoping to return in glory only to find themselves at the butt end of Paddy jokes, and the suspicion engendered by the fallout from the Troubles. With big wages, came big drinking; and with big drinking came destitution. I would know them at a glance, I found them everywhere and it broke my heart.

'A Hard Man To Follow' is written out of sympathy for an England that found it hard to follow the waxing lyrical of a people with a natural turn of phrase who hail from a culture with such a rich mythology. Sometimes it seems to me that our eloquence and our sense of fun may have been misinterpreted as hocus pocus, at best. It is amazing to think that inside ten to fifteen years to be Irish in England has changed so positively and has accelerated since the peace process came to pass.

I learned to write in London. I found a part of myself there that I could not have found anywhere else and, whenever I return, I feel the warmth of coming home.

9

Guiding Star

When I was nineteen, I started playing in bars and folk clubs. The first gig was a holiday season three nights a week in the Pirates Den, Crosshaven, County Cork – £5 a night and all the drink I could manage. A few miles up the coast was another wonderful establishment known as Bunnyconnellen, and here I played with a friend from my early teenage summers in Myrtleville, Owen Hunter O'Brien – now known as Obi Hunter – a recording artist with two albums to his credit. Bunny's, as it was always known, was renowned for its singsongs and hospitality. It had a piano bar for older patrons in the inner sanctum, and a guitar circle in the outer bar for the younger ones. It was a fantastic place and time. The proprietors were Neil Porteous, a Scotsman who had settled and married in Ireland, and his wife Mary. They were bright and generous people and were very good to Owen and me.

Owen and I then pooled our resources and became Huntermac – we grew long hair and beards, wore beads, flares and platform boots. All we were short of was a manager. Enter Bomber DJ Daniels who, within a month or so, booked us a support slot, opening for the legendary Planxty in the Savoy Limerick and the Savoy Cork. We arrived for our sound check at 4.30 in the afternoon in Limerick only to discover that the support slot was advertised as Barry Moore, now known as Luca Bloom. Still, we were allowed to play and we were paid. We went on first and played a set of Crosbie, Stills, Nash & Young songs, four or five originals, and Owen's special rendition of the Scottish ballad 'Jordie'. Next up was Barry, who impressed us with his finger-picking style and his version of 'Michael In The Garden'. Then there was a twenty-minute interval. During this time, we wandered around the new and magical world of backstage activity. Planxty came out on stage and lifted the place with two or three tunes, and then the world stopped and – from 'Only Her Rivers Run Free' to 'The Cliffs Of Duneen', from 'Flow Sweet River Flow' to the 'Well Below The Valley O' – this was Christy Moore.

The next time I met Christy, he was singing in the Meeting Place, Dorset Street, Dublin, in 1978 and there was revolution in the air. Sincere in the good. Every man must have something he follows – something that serves him as a lodestar. He who follows with conviction the beautiful and the good may feel himself strengthened by this saying (Hexagram 17 Sui/Following I ching).

I went home and wrote this song.

Guiding Star

I found you in the spotlight
Throwing dreams across the stage

And the shadows danced
With the sweet romance
With the hunger and the rage
And your songs of revolution
And your songs of losing love
I knew well the pain
In your clear blue eyes
As you sung of a God above

And you carried a flame for the people
And you carried it through the night
And if you could find a way out of there
You wouldn't leave alone and that's all right

Chorus *Sing your songs*
Be what you are
Carry the flame
Guiding star

You're a soldier, a fine soldier
You're giving it all your best
You come home from the wars
And you wear the scars
Like medals on your vest
I still see you in the spotlight
Throwing dreams across the stage
How the shadows danced

With the sweet romance
With the hunger and the rage

Chorus   *Sing your songs*
          Be what you are
          Carry the flame
          Guiding star

10

A Letter to Hughie

A Letter to Hughie

In the age of disposable talent
Where the keepers decide what you palate
While they put to the roads what's forever
And they blow out the bubbles and feathers

But the flame that has fired us together
In the bars or the halls or wherever
Where we soar at the ivory gates
Of a warm and a sensual sea
Where I still belong to you
And you still belong to me
Forever I defy you
To put an ear to the heart of the soulman

To throw an eye on the human condition
Not just the Sky Channel jive
It's not canned man, it's live
It's a pathetic and censored rendition
You've got it down on a par with the rag mag
And under the keeper's thumb, these princes must be
What these princes must be
But we claim a place by the drum
By the drum is forever, and forever I defy you

I first met Big Hughie in LA about fifteen years ago – he was an overweight, middle-aged, cigar-smoking maker and breaker of plastic pop stars, with a reputation for the ladies, white powder and fine wines. I met him again in the early 1990s in New York while attending the New Music Seminar. With legendary success under his belt, he walked by looking more like Julius Caesar than the manager of a pop idol.

Another of his weaknesses, which at one point affected me directly, was his absolute delight in letting fly with untrue and defamatory remarks about anyone outside of his elite and tight-knit circle. Later I was to discover that the reputation Hughie had, and carelessly flaunted, was merely a façade, and bore no relation to who Hughie truly was.

In saying all of this, and in writing 'A Letter To Hughie', I want to make it clear that I am a child of the radio, and the magic of pop music and, to this day, when I hear the real thing, my heart soars. In my own song-writing, no matter how deep I go, my sensibility is still predominately pop.

11

As I Leave Behind Néidín

As I Leave Behind Néidín

As I leave behind Néidín
It's like purple splashed on green
And my soul is strangely fed
Through the winding hills ahead
As she plays a melody
On wind and streams for me

Chorus   *Won't you remember*
Won't you remember
Won't you remember me

And we wind and climb and fall
Like the greatest waltz of all

Float across the floor
Her sweet breath outside the door
And it's time that I was gone
Across the silver tear

Chorus   *Won't you remember*
Won't you remember
Won't you remember me

As I leave behind Néidín
In the hall where we had been
Rhododendrons in her hair
In the mountain-scented air
I still feel her spirit song
Across the silver tear

Chorus   *Won't you remember*
Won't you remember
Won't you remember me

The genial Darby Crowley is a brother of legendary folk singer Jimmy Crowley, and it was in Darby's company that I set to work on 'As I Leave Behind Néidín'. We travelled in Darby's van through Coolea up over the county bounds between Cork and Kerry, climbing and falling, rhododendron everywhere. We were on our way to Kenmare – *Néidín, as Gaeilge* – to the *Cibeál Cincíse*, a great festival run by the mighty Joe Thoma. It was a wonderful feast of art, music, dance and craic.

Joe worked tirelessly putting these festivals together, which were of great benefit to the town. Obviously the place would be littered at the end of these Whit Bank Holiday weekends, and some locals on their way to mass on Sunday morning had a little difficulty in negotiating the bodies sprawled in sleeping bags on the main street. First thing on Monday morning, aggrieved inhabitants would lay into Joe, who then, in his frustration to explain his predicament, would mimic the complainers, 'Yourself and your fecking feshtival. The town is filthay.'

On Monday lunchtime, Darby and I went to Crowley's bar, owned by the kindly and wise Mrs Crowley, who kept a great house for traditional music sessions. We went for something to steady the nerves, and to listen to the sublime fiddle playing of Seamus and Manus Maguire. We listened for an hour in delight, finished our drinks and headed for home. I looked out the back window as we drove away and there, in black and white, the sign for *Néidín*, a starting point. When I got home with my scribbled notes I finished the song, my first on piano. When I woke the following morning, in my bedsit in Lavanagh, Ballintemple in Cork, and switched on the tape of the finished song, I declared I had written my pension.

12

My Singing Bird

The People of West Cork and Kerry

My Singing Bird

My singing bird lies dead and cold
His colours were too bright
Too bright and too bold
Golden wings fanned and frozen
No more to herald the light
The light from out of darkness springing
A blue-and-gold delight

Oh that singing bird did heal my heart
Did heal my friend and foe
And did not set each apart
He braved the rain and raging storm
And the hungry, winter snow
Each note is a symbol
If you follow, you will know

Chorus   *Shall I run to the garden and lift him from the snow*
And breathe into his mouth life's elixir
Or is it too late for a rescue remedy
To save the life in him
To save the song in me

My singing bird lies dead and cold
His colours were too bright
Too bright and too bold
They would whisper in the groves in darkness
All the creatures of the night
That blue-and-golden singing bird
He was their hearts' delight

If that singing bird could rise again
And tell us what he's seen
And sing of where he's been
His golden wings would shine and shimmer
And sparkle in the light

Oh let it not be death
But let it be respite

Chorus   *Shall I run to the garden and lift him from the snow*
             And breathe into his mouth, life's elixir
             Or is it too late for a rescue remedy
             To save the life in him
             To save the song in me
             My singing bird
             My blue-and-golden bird
             My singing bird
             My blue-and-golden bird

In the late 1990s, when I was living in Wicklow, I received a tape of ten songs and a letter from a girl, who I did not know, named Carmel McCarron from Killorglin, County Kerry. On the tape cover, she had dedicated these songs to me but I lost the letter and could not reply. I would like to take this opportunity to acknowledge the kindness of her gesture. Some days later, I listened to the tape in its entirety and decided I would write a dedication to the people of West Cork and Kerry, a sort of 'Homes Of Donegal' down south. I wrote the title on the top of a blank page and stared at it for a long time. I was stricken by a feeling of absolute terror that there wasn't a song left in me. For the first time since I started writing songs twenty years earlier, I hadn't written anything new for well over a year.

I had never put down roots; I had stayed here and there, my address was Side Of The Road, The World, and not too long anywhere. Then, in the 1990s, a house was brought to my attention by an auctioneer friend, John Barry. It was in Wicklow and had a stable yard with land. Apart from the house itself, the property was very rundown and required a lot of work. Before the deal was closed, I received a call from a Swedish man, Ola Ballack, who asked me if I would stable and graze thirty foals for him and I agreed without hesitation. I worked tirelessly from dawn to dusk and, even though looking after the foals was a labour of love, along with the other tasks involved, the work was daunting and, for the first six months, I worked seven days a week. As a result of this, for the first time in well over twenty years, music was to take a back seat for the next year or two.

My love of horses goes right back to my childhood, when my brother Dan and I had two ponies, and later I used to go around to horse fairs and gymkhanas in the summer holidays with Gerald Coakley, a well-known horse-and-pony dealer. Then, when I was fifteen, I went to work as a trainee for the legendary racehorse trainer Vincent O'Brien at Ballydoyle, Rosegreen, County Tipperary, for seven shillings and sixpence a week and my keep.

This was a most magical time. It was the end of Sir Ivor's reign and the beginning of Nijinsky's – a racehorse who had been called after the great Russian dancer who, on his deathbed, had promised that he would return to earth as a stallion – and I made it my business to have sat on the backs of both, two of the greatest horses of our time.

I suffered a very bad accident at Ballydoyle, when a yearling filly reared up and fell backwards on top of me. As she came back, I leaned to one side and I can still hear the crack of my femur breaking in the early morning fog with a string of some of the most valuable horses in the world walking

79

around me. I returned to Ballydoyle for another year after six months in traction before moving on to Newmarket, one of the world's great racing centres, where I worked for Billy O'Gorman until I was nineteen. There I took out my apprentice jockey's licence, and had a few rides in maiden races and handicaps. I enjoyed Newmarket very much, and all its racing life. However, even at this young age, I had to waste to make the weight and when the first decent horse I was to ride, a good handicapper named Gold Strike, was pulled from the Lincoln due to an injury, and I had wasted hard in order to ride him, my disappointment brought me face to face with the inevitable and I returned home.

On returning to Ireland, I worked for my father in his garage, accounts and transport business for a while, but soon withdrawals from my beloved horses kicked in. So I got a job, riding work for the great horseman Fergie Sutherland, trainer of Imperial Call in Killinardrish, County Cork. It was for Fergie that I rode my last race, in Mallow, on a horse named Ballymackeera.

Twenty-odd years later, sitting in my kitchen in Wicklow, and in despair at having dried up, I walked to the window and looked out and there, on a blanket of snow, lay a little dead bird. 'Shall I run to the garden and lift him from the snow and breath into his mouth life's elixir, or is it too late for a rescue remedy, to save the life in him, to save the song in me?'

I finished 'My Singing Bird' at one sitting and, shortly afterwards, 'The People Of West Cork And Kerry', a tribute to those people and to Carmel McCarron in particular.

In my times of trouble, I would head for West Cork or Kerry and take the waters of kindness. The well is there for all. No matter how many come, all will find what they need, for the well is dependable. It has a spring and never runs dry (Hexagram 48 Ching/The Well I Ching).

The People of West Cork and Kerry

It seems to me the people of West Cork and Kerry
Seem to understand best the ways of my soul
They seem to recognise the healing ways of a young man
Born into pain and, for the song, had to roam
And now though still not old, I live alone in the garden
The pen it is slow, and my heart is at rest
And when I see the world, I see a world without turmoil
In all things I see now, I look for the best

Chorus   *I know all the towns*
And I know all the places
And I have kissed your lips
And I have held your hand
Been all around the world
And have not found such graces
For the people of West Cork and Kerry
The people of West Cork and Kerry were grand

But when I was a young man, the world was heavy on me
You gave me plain talk and you made me feel blessed
You gave me the magic of all that went before me
And when I needed to lay low, you gave me the nest
So it seems to me the people of West Cork and Kerry
That, even in a wild heart, they seem to find the best

Chorus   *I know all the towns*
And I know all the places
And I have kissed your lips
And I have held your hand
Been all around the world
And have not found such graces
For the people of West Cork and Kerry
The people of West Cork and Kerry were grand

13

For Maurice Desmond

For Maurice Desmond

There's a hand at an easel
Trying not to disguise
The subject's dense matter
Fearing loss to the eyes
So he splits one into two
Like a number eleven
And he's painting a rope
From the Earth up to Heaven
Rising with the eagle
And the sad, silver salmon
These are the eyes of the Lamb of God

I wrote 'For Maurice Desmond' for the opening of an exhibition of paintings by the great painter Maurice Desmond in the mid-1980s. I had admired Maurice from a distance long before I met him, a romantic and heroic-looking figure with an Irish wolfhound at his side. In those days, I had heard many stories about his legendary sense of justice. One that particularly exemplifies this was the case of a farmer who had advertised for a rabbit that carried, and could spread, the horrendous disease myxomatosis – a common practice of farmers at that time, but thankfully no longer the case. Maurice took the trouble to find such an unfortunate creature, brought it to the farmer's house, and there in the kitchen took the rabbit and a shotgun from a hessian sack and, with the heart of light and the darkness of justice, shot the rabbit, ending its misery and the potential for so much more suffering. I imagine the farmer got the message.

Maurice and his partner Deirdre Meeney, who was a wonderful batik artist and who has sadly passed away since, showed me great kindness and gave my work uplifting encouragement. I remember well, and with great warmth, the times we spent together. Happier company I've never known.

85

14

The Greatest Song of All

The Greatest Song of All

The autumn rust returns to dust
A promise made in ancient trust
Her olden gown of flowing hues
Her nakedness of winter blues
Long, snowy-white whiteness
Now exposed
Surely to these arms, no lover goes
But one did come, and one did sing
The seed of Heaven, the joyous spring
The hallelujah's golden way
The Lord Himself, a summer's day

I wrote these words in the early 1990s while driving from Dublin to Cork and listening to a tape of Vivaldi's 'Four Seasons'. This is a very short piece, which I recorded on to a dictaphone en route. My plan was to elaborate and extend the work when I got back to Dublin but, on writing it down, it struck me as being complete. My belief has always been that a song lyric can never be too short but can often be too long.

15

Harlem

Harlem

I want to go back to Harlem
And walk with Johnny in the park
And take my breakfast with the colours
Of the world
And lose this crippling dark
That has followed me
Like a gypsy priest of a gypsy people
'Till I came to be free as the wind
Running through the streets of Harlem
With the matadors in the darkened doors of Harlem
I hear the drum of the rhythm people
I hear the heel and castanets

I hear the birth of an Ancient Order
And the brogues dancing to the half set
Gospel songs, Lord, to thee
Led by the priests of her people
A far cry to be free as the wind
She's still the unnamed rose of Harlem
With the matadors and the shamrock shores of Harlem
And from the land of the matador – sweet Rosita
And from the far shamrock shore – sad Roisín
I asked at soul's door
But none could redeem her
Their words come to me now
Their words come to me now

Chorus   *They bury many roses*
      They bury many roses in Harlem
      They bury many roses
      They bury many roses in Harlem

The first time I travelled to America was in 1987 and it was with DeDanann. I had been introduced to Alec Finn and the traditional fiddle player Frankie Gavin, both of DeDanann, by a friend from my younger days, Colm Murphy, an excellent bodhrán player and also a fine artist. Colm is the son of Seamus Murphy, the famous sculptor and author of the little classic *Stone*

Mad. I had been involved in the production of their album *A Jacket of Batteries* and had played some concerts with them in Ireland, singing some of my own songs. 'The Bright Blue Rose', 'The Mad Lady And Me' and 'As I Leave Behind Néidín' were all beautifully DeDanannised.

The band was about to embark on a tour of America and asked me to join them. Colm and I travelled by bus to Galway and we rehearsed a set of songs and tunes. I might mention that, up to this point, I had never backed tunes except very casually, so I wrote out all the chord progressions and carried the scraps of paper right across America. We played twenty-three venues in twenty-one days and I opened every show with my usual set, and then continued to play with the band till the end of the night. As the saying goes, they were the best of times, and the worst. When they were bad it was like being hurled into Dante's Inferno, and when they were good it was like going to heaven on a jumbo jet. When Frankie kicked into turbo overdrive we all just flew on his magic carpet.

During this trip, I met another friend, John O'Mahony – from Bantry, County Cork – in New York where he wrote for the *Irish Voice* and later the *New York Post*. The next time I returned to New York to attend the Music Seminar in 1990, I stayed in Harlem with John, who shared a house there with an art dealer, Ginita, a quick-witted black girl, who, without knowing it, became my guide through this song. Harlem's vibrancy and colourfulness fascinated me. Then I was to discover that, before the black peoples and Hispanics settled there, the district had originally been an Irish ghetto and I was told that when the Irish workers on the docks felt threatened by the incoming black workers, a blood bath ensued. I hung my head at the description of this. I continued to paint my picture of Harlem in my quest for the third and unnamed Rose. Suffice to say, they bury many roses in Harlem.

16

Diamond Days · State of Heart

'Diamond Days' was a parting gift, at the end of a holiday romance, to a sweetheart who played Lauren Bacall to my twitching Bogart. The song was written in the dim light of the Carmel Hotel, John's Street, Kilkenny, twenty minutes before going on stage.

'Diamond Days' and 'State Of Heart' are for me rare examples of romantic love songs of the kind that only the young can write.

Diamond Days

I have written this song
For you to take with you
When you go away
Something to sing and slowly swing to
On your colder days

I have made a start
With a verse and a chorus
And the rest I'll leave to you
And when next I see your smiling face
We might sing it right through

Chorus I'll be your sweetheart always
And I'll love the memory of the Diamond Days
I'll keep a candle burning
Till we sing again the Diamond Days

If the words don't rhyme
Then I will forgive you
That won't be the crime
But the staring space
Upon the page
That might look like mine
I have made a start
With a verse and a chorus
And the rest I'll leave to you
And when next I see your smiling face
We might sing it right through

Chorus I'll be your sweetheart always
And I'll love the memory of the Diamond Days
I'll keep a candle burning
Till we sing again the Diamond Days

State of Heart

Something must be done
About my state of heart
I woke with it this morning
And now it's nearly dark
I don't know what to do
The blame must lie with you

Chorus *I'm falling, falling, I'm falling*
And you're living in a glass jar
I'm falling, falling, I'm falling
And you're living in a glass jar

Sitting in your place
Inside your window draped in lace
I feel my fingers scratch the pane
Didn't want to fall in love again
My heart is in your hands
Queen of these love lands

Something must be done
About my state of heart
Throne stands empty in the dawn
Lies empty in the dark
My heart is in your hands
Queen of these love lands

Chorus   *I'm falling, falling, I'm falling*
And you're living in a glass jar
I'm falling, falling, I'm falling
And you're living in a glass jar

17

On Another Day

On Another Day

Hey little brother
The winds of the world
Have ruffled your soft and weakened wings
And though my hands don't reach you
As I look into your eyes
I can see the film
Disappointment brings

I know it's rained
Upon your fire of dreams
And the games you've been playing
Just weren't what they seemed
How can I tell you

Don't bang your head against the wall
A wall I'm banging and praying might fall

Chorus   *Your time*
Will come on another day
Your dreams
Will flame and in the fire will play
On another day
On another day

I know it's hard to understand
There are no flying angels
Who come to lend a hand
No smiling faces lined for you to meet
Looks like that in twisted glass
From the kind side
Of the street

Chorus   *Your time*
Will come on another day
Your dreams
Will flame and in the fire will play
On another day
On another day

100

'On Another Day' was written for my brother Rory. Like myself, Rory shouldered independence at a very early age and, though of tender years, weathered the winds of the world without complaint. Though I was still young myself when I wrote this song, I could see the potential dangers that lay ahead of him. On reflection, he has negotiated the obstacle course that is life at least as well as the rest of us. Rory now lives near Macroom in County Cork. He is a jewellery maker, working with deerhorn, silver and gold, but his great passion is for handcrafted bog oak. Rory is also a fine stonemason. He attended the Crawford Art College, Cork, as did my sister Marion and my brother Sean.

Sean, a fine draughtsman, was born with a sketchpad and pencil attached and is a professional artist, painter and figurative sculptor. He has many public works to his name and his seven-and-a-half-foot bronze of the legendary hurler Christy Ring that stands at Cork Airport is featured in this book. He was also commissioned to do a piece of similar dimensions of President Bill Clinton on the occasion of his visit to Ireland and that piece now stands at Ballybunion.

So, while I wrote this song with my brother Rory in mind, I was also mindful of Sean, who took the hard road and suffered for his art.

101

18

Christian Telephone

Christian Telephone

Tongues of fire, and hearts of stone
No reply on the Christian telephone
Lose the Word, and all is lost
Christ it's such a double cross
But I'd never thought they'd turn away
And leave him to die lonely, sad and blue
No, I never thought they'd turn away
And leave him to die lonely

Retribution's wrath in fusion
In the holy minds of wild illusion
Hoof upon the hallowed marble
Vain men, like peacocks, warble

But I never thought they'd turn away
And leave him to die lonely, sad and blue
And no, I never thought they'd turn away
And leave him to die lonely

I am not exactly sure when 'Christian Telephone' was written, but it was while watching the *Late Late Show* on RTÉ 1 that I was taken by a guest, Fr Lynch, who spoke about the treatment meted out by the Catholic Church in America to its priests who had contracted the Aids virus. They were not treated in a very sympathetic fashion.

The same absence of Christian charity and moral backbone has become increasingly apparent in the workings of the Church with regard to the evil perpetrated by its paedophile priests. It must be said that almost all the clergy, from the highest to the lowest, knew about this vileness and still the cloth maintains its unholy silence, a silence which clearly denotes a corrupt institution. Let me draw an analogy. I stand by a stream and watch a child drown. Standing close to the riverbank, I could reach him easily, and pull him to safety, instead, I stand there and let him drown, saying it wasn't I who threw him in.

All of this said, I still passionately believe in the necessity for the existence of a Christian ministry and society, to provide a house where we can collectively talk to our maker in times of tribulation and jubilation.

19

Wonder Child

Wonder Child

This child he means the world to me
There is no more enchanted
A child can take this place to ruin
And magically enhance it

I see him in a golden room
With the Book of Life before him
Strange instruments upon his charts
And the crystal glow inside him

Chorus *He's your Wonder Child*
And my dreams come true

You've searched all of your life
I see him now flying over the universe

This child will build a violin
One will follow the traveller's love
Another will the bow apply
To reach the One above

I see her in a golden room
With the moon and stars about her
Her simple smile is Heaven's gate
With the Queen of all beside her

Chorus   *She's your Wonder Child*
And my dreams come true
You've searched all of your life
I see them now flying over the universe

On wings of love
Flying over the universe

In 1992, I was approached by a friend, Sally-Ann O'Reilly, to write a song and a piece of music for a promotional video she was making. The aim of the project was to raise awareness and funds for an awe-inspiring walk to be undertaken by Dr John Scully. He planned to walk coast-to-coast across America – from San Diego to Maine, 5,000 miles in total. For eight months and one week he walked 25 miles a day, and this when he was in his late sixties, in my opinion an achievement that must be viewed with the greatest admiration. He had set up the Dr Pamela Scully Memorial Fund, in his wife's name, addressing the theme of 'Give a child a chance'. This foundation has already addressed the high-school educational needs of underprivileged Native American children in the US, children in the Philippines and rural Zimbabwe and, closer to home, handicapped children in Galway. I wrote the song 'Wonder Child' to promote this project and the song was recorded in Windmill Lane Studios. I produced it under the watchful eye of Sally-Ann, and we were joined by the choral group Anúna who sang an arrangement written by Michael McGlynn, a composer and arranger whose genius had not then been fully recognised.

'Wonder Child' has been used over the years to benefit children in need. Mary Black and her husband Joe O'Reilly, head of Dara Records, generously donated Mary's version of the song to the charity fundraising organisation Concern. Mary's version also features on the album *Russian Lullaby*, which was produced and co-ordinated by the talented Jeanette Byrne for the charity To Russia with Love, an organisation founded in Dublin to aid the abandoned and orphaned children in western Russia.

When I set about writing this song, I could not find a starting point. Nothing worked. As I had become increasingly more interested in self-venture, I had been listening to a tape of John Bradshaw, who has written some ground-breaking recovery and self-help books. My tape copy had material on one side only, I believed, as it was a home recording given to me by a friend. I had been listening to it while driving along the Crosshaven—

Cork road until I pulled up outside the sub-tropical explosion of tree and plant life that is my parents' home at Curraheen Drive in Bishopstown.

It was about 6.15 on a winter's evening and the rain started to pour down, the tape flipped over to the B-side, I heard the sound of a synthesiser pad, behind the speaking voice. The voice said, 'You are looking at a white number three on a black curtain, now it's two, now one.' Then I was guided through an interior journey by instructions like these: 'There is a door,' the voice said, 'leading on to a long corridor and you walk through it. On your left-hand side there is the first of several doors. Open it, and inside you find all your classmates from your last year at school. Further down the corridor, in another classroom, there you are, eleven years old.' The voice directed me from room to room until I came to the infant classroom and there I could clearly see Miss Ahern, my first teacher at Glasheen Primary School. The guidance continued, 'At the end of the corridor is another white door which leads out on to the garden in front of the home where you spent your early childhood. Sitting on the doorstep is a little child who has been frozen in time and has been waiting, all of your life, for you to come and get him. Lift him up and tell him that, of all the people who have ever left him, you never will. Now as you walk away from the house you both turn and wave goodbye to your parents, who are standing content and smiling in the doorway.

'Now take the child to a higher place, a perfectly still lake cradled on the side of a mountain. Here you meet the ancients, an old man and woman both with long lustrous grey hair. They greet the child with delight and celebration and they both leave with joyous hearts. "I must go now, but I will return tomorrow," you tell this child, "and, of all the people who have ever left you, I never will." The child shrinks to the size of a button in the palm of your

109

hand, and you put him in your heart until the following day.' The tape stopped, my face wet and tears ran like rain across the windscreen. I had found the place of the child, a place of wonder and accidental healing.

20

Switzerland in Snow

Switzerland in Snow

When you're strange and a stranger
In the strangest place
And you're facing the Everest on the Eiger Face
Where you marvel, marvel upwards, at the beautiful eves
On the ledge, in the company of continental thieves

I met a woman in the ape house
She seemed to know my name
She was great, and she was awful
But I loved her just the same
Then a dog, a great composer
To shift the play, he changed the game
And traded gold for nickel silver

And blew it all, on long-lost fame
And on the streets below
The milk and honey flows
The milk and honey, all that money
Switzerland in Snow

I met a cat he spoke in English
He spoke in drink, and he spoke in soul
I liked his style, he was a soldier
We shared a common lack of goal
He also marvelled, marvelled upwards at the beautiful eves
On the ledge in the company of continental thieves
And on the streets below
The milk and honey flows
The milk and honey, all that money
Switzerland in Snow

I returned home to my parents' house at the age of thirty (as I mentioned when writing about 'The Contender' and 'That Face') and slowly began to find my feet. I struck a deal with Richard Burke, the then manager of Jury's Hotel in Cork, who kindly gave me an affordable daily rate for the Leisure Centre, where I did a workout, swim and sauna most days. Being still new to recovery, I was brittle and a little edgy, and these activities helped a lot.

My socialising now for the most part was done in coffee shops, and I went out of my way to avoid my old haunts. But I desperately missed the Café Lorca. Here my friends would gather after closing time and we would sing, dance, laugh, cry and drink red wine with insatiable zest. Bill and Bernie were the proprietors and many's the morning they let me out into the blinding sunlight of Washington Street, still trying to negotiate one last drink. The problem with avoiding these places was that I was now without the bright company that I had enjoyed so much. 'What's wrong with Jimmy Mac? Sure he wasn't a big drinker. If *he* has a problem we're all in big trouble.'

I was now beginning to get a few gigs, so I handed all income from them over to my father to manage, and began to accumulate enough for posters and to budget for what might be loosely described as transport. One day before the long-awaited carriage materialised, I remember heading off from the bus station at Parnell Place in Cork to play at Seán Óg's pub in Ballyshannon, County Donegal. The bus departed from the Cork depot at eight in the morning and arrived at Ballyshannon shortly before nine that evening. Then straight into action. First check out the PA system. Then a quick guitar/vocal sound check, coffee, a sandwich and back on stage by 9.30, where I played on a little wooden square in the middle of a large room. By ten o'clock the place was chock-a-block, very loud and boisterous – that was the way it was with a lot of non-folk club gigs. An angel whisked me off to Donegal town to a late-night session at The Diamond, and I headed for home the following morning.

I recounted my journey to my father on my return and he decided to make up the difference with regard to purchasing the previously mentioned transport. By now I had started a residency in the Grape Vine room of the Metropole Hotel. I was also doing two or three other gigs a week and, before long, the chilly winds of insolvency began to slacken, for the time being at least.

By now I was itching to record an album so badly I could hardly sleep but, as I could not get a deal, I had to raise the funds by myself and find a studio and a producer. Then a friend, the painter Ramie Leahy from Kilkenny, put me in touch with a Swiss musician/producer, Martin Fischer, aka Chicken, who lived in Aarau, near Zürich in Switzerland. Chicken duly found a studio, Greenwood Studios, in Nuningen, near Basel, owned by Glenn Miller of 'Pop Music' fame.

The plan was hatched. Now, how to raise the money? A friend in need is a friend indeed as I discovered when I approached Des Blaire, who proved to be a friend in deed and lent me £6,000, a lot of money in those days. Donal and Cecilia Gallagher lent me the same amount and my sincerest thanks goes to them for their belief in me, their generosity and patience.

My father had advised me against embarking on a such a venture at a vulnerable time saying, 'Jim Boy, you may be dry, but you are not yet sober. Can't you wait a while longer?' But I could not and, eventually, £18,000 was spent and the project failed. I had made a monumental blunder. All initial decisions were mine and I will not apportion blame. I was unable to live with the result and I returned to Ireland, trying to deny my inner voices, but finally succumbed to an extended lost weekend.

Returning to Aarau, my guilt and shame weighed heavy on me, but I dusted myself off, playing bars, railway stations and the occasional club. Sonia Ott, a friend who worked in a music bar, The Affencasten, made it possible for me to use the piano function room, so that I could write during the day. Here I wrote 'Switzerland In Snow', a surreal pen-picture of my trials in the land of milk and honey, where the money tree still grows. I suppose I would not be the first to find some kind of glory in failure.

115

21

Katie

It was in Aarau that I also finished 'Katie'. I had started this song some time before, with a working title of 'The Room', but it didn't have a chorus or a third verse. The chorus subject matter was borrowed from the lifescape of another person (thanks for the clearance, Declan), but the sentiment was perfect, and seemed to complete the song. Then, with this new aspect in place, I got a final flash of inspiration for the last verse with an image from Newgrange and the makings of a first crossover hit for the fast-rising star of Mary Black. This, along with my growing body of recorded works, would soon be my redemption in clearing my debt, which I'm glad to say I eventually did.

Katie

The tumbling curls of green
By the stained-glass streaming light
And a yellow-coloured lampshade

Used to keep us up all night
The smile upon your face and the tears upon your cheek
The night sky on the window and your
Heart calling out to me

Chorus *Come running home again Katie*
Come running home again
Cross my heart and hope to die
Should I cause another tear from your eye

The mirror that won't talk
And your nightgown on the door
And the old pedal Singer just won't sing no more
You could roll the reels for hours
From the movie of this book
It's a question mark on this heart of mine
Sends an elder back to look

Chorus *Come running home again Katie*
Come running home again
Cross my heart and hope to die
Should I cause another tear from your eye

Now I'm looking through a tunnel
Back into the room
With the genius of the Druid
When the sunlight floods the tomb

And I'm never going back there
And I couldn't anyway
For though I made the great escape
I never got away

Chorus   *Come running home again Katie*
Come running home again
Cross my heart and hope to die
Should I cause another tear from your eye

22

Adam at the Window

Adam at the Window

Adam's at the window
Staring at the apple trees on fire
Waiting for the windfall
That brings the smile of kings and their desires
Door blows in behind him
A floral-pattern summer dress so gay
Burning in the sunlight
Too late to wait
For darkness won't delay
To steal her cherry lips away
So while the careless tongues of sunlight
Slowly trickle down

The curve of hips, her fingertips
In kissing sips we drown
In kissing sips we drown
And Adam will have his way

Adam's on the island
Living in the land of love
Shadows lurk around him
Drunk on the royal jelly of pure love
Full and ripe the fruit hang
For when the prince arrives, he will want more
And more and more he will drink from the canvas cup
The son of a swan will then
Lose his plume array
And he will wear a New Age suit
And haunt the joints in town
And play a silver magic flute
And call his lover down
And call his lover down
And Adam will have his way

Adam's at the easel
Painting in the wrinkles and the grey
Waiting for November
Easy with the darkness and the day
Smiles a tear of gladness
And Adam's at the window once again

Burning in the sunlight
Too late to wait
For darkness won't delay
To steal her cherry lips away
So while the careless tongues of sunlight
Slowly trickle down
The curve of hips, her fingertips
In kissing sips we drown
In kissing sips we drown
And Adam will have his way

One night, while playing at The Affencasten, a tall, young man accompanied by a beautiful, young, blonde woman, came up to me, handed me a business card, asked my name, and said, 'Call me tomorrow.' The following morning I phoned him and we arranged to meet in Grenchen. Claude Jufer was his name and he was a 25-year-old, self-made millionaire. He had made his fortune as a property speculator, but he ran a music promotions and management business on the side. In typical Swiss fashion, we made a contract and, within a couple of days, I moved into an apartment in Solothurn, one of the oldest towns in Europe, a quiet and very beautiful place. Claude was a really good drummer, played keyboard quite well and loved music and everything about the music business. He was an only child and the only evidence of family that I ever saw was his grandfather, whom he loved dearly. Sometimes we went to see him on Thursdays for lunch. It was great.

Claude loved to win and, night after night, we battled over the backgammon board for the childish title of King of the Night. He was generous to a fault; what was his was mine, even down to driving his highly prized Porsche.

It was an idyllic sanctuary but, by now, I really needed to record something, even a single for a start. I thought 'Adam At The Window' might be the one. I went to Claude and said, 'I want to record a single and put it out in Ireland.'

'OK,' he said. 'Where and with whom do you want to do this?'

Chancing my arm, I said, 'With Phil Manzanero of Roxy Music in his studio in Surrey.'

'OK, we'll do that,' he replied. Within a week it had been set up so we travelled to England – Claude, his beautiful companion and me – then, after the recording, Claude and I went to Ireland.

124

The three days in Phil Manzanero's studio were just fantastic, he used brilliant studio players, I loved his production, and it is a memory I cherish still.

'Adam At The Window' was my third single, and it was put out on Dennis Desmond's Solid Records label. It was picked up and played by Pat Kenny on his morning radio show and, eventually, got great airplay. Pat is a man with a good ear and a fair heart who has opened the way for many as he certainly did for me.

'Adam' is a lyric that I love and will never tire of. It was written on one of my visits back to Cork from Switzerland during the week of the Cork Folk Festival. The singer-songwriter John Spillane and his then partner Jo Allen, aka Jo Diamond, a Cork-based painter, lived in a house called El Oro. They were heading off to play some dates in Portugal and asked me if I would house-sit El Oro while they were gone, though I think this was more an act of generosity than of necessity. They were expecting a baby shortly after their return from this trip and Adam was the name I had given this unborn child.

One day, out of the blue, a friend of mine, Sylvia Andrivè, from Paris appeared at the door wearing a beautiful, floral-patterned dress. We went to see most of the festival's offerings and we rambled the town in that golden and late-summer sunshine. In the garden behind El Oro was an apple tree with flaming-red apples and already Adam at the window. Throughout the house there was evidence of a painter, large canvases with bold paintings, some unfinished – the art of Adam's mother, 'the canvas cup' of the song. His father was a swan living in a world that could not maintain the high code of swans.

I loved the world during this week and saw the never-endingness of things so clearly through my attempt to capture life's perfect circle. But, as John Lennon said, 'Life is what happens when you're busy making plans', and Adam arrived – a lovely girl named Lesley! How could this happen? I was devastated, so I decided to look up what Adam actually meant. Lo and behold it comes from the Hebrew and means 'from God' and stands for neither 'man' nor 'woman' but for 'person' and I said, 'Yes, there is a God, and thanks be to God.'

It was during this same week that Mandy Murphy, who sang backing vocals in Mary Black's band, played me a live version of 'Katie', and I knew we were in business. El Oro had certainly lived up to its name.

23

The Bright Blue Rose

O n returning to Switzerland, I wrote like a man possessed. Something had changed in me. I just did not feel easy, I was lost in a deep pool and waiting for the river to rise, writing page after page of subconscious flow, with no idea what it meant. I returned home to my parent's house and my health gave in. It was nothing life threatening; I was suffering from a condition that was the result of being run down. Still, I felt desperately ill and was in need of a reasonably simple medical procedure, so a hospital bed was booked.

This was during the notorious hospital cutbacks of that time in the 1980s. On arrival, the overnight bed was not available, and the surgical procedure was carried out on a trolley in a small storeroom, half full with cardboard boxes of medical supplies. An hour later, I was given a cup of tea and was told I could go. As I walked through Accident and Emergency towards the door, I felt faint and collapsed, but finding my feet as quickly as possible, I made my way to the reception nearby expecting to be whisked to care. They called for a taxi.

During the following week of recuperation, a songwriter friend, Martin Egan from Dingle, came to stay with us for a few days. On Good Friday morning he moved on, and, on that same day, I had words with my father. I had been trying to shape my litany into a verse and was like a hair trigger.

After my disagreement with my father, I decided to head for Kenmare to some celebration or other but, by Saturday evening in the Kenmare Bay Hotel, I felt very ill, so I booked a room and checked in. Then a woman, a healer who shall remain nameless, approached me and said, 'You look very unwell. Let me give you a blast.' We went to my hotel room where she asked me to sit on a chair and take my shirt off. I felt unbelievable heat coming from her hands onto my back, even though she wasn't making physical contact with me. Within twenty minutes or so I got a surge of energy. I returned to the celebrations where I sang four or five songs with Chris Meehan and his Red-Neck Friends, if my memory serves me well. Before going to bed, this healer gave me one last blast and I awoke on Easter Sunday morning totally recovered. From the bedside locker, I picked up my ever-present notepad with the work in progress, and wrote the completing lines: 'One bright blue rose outlives all those/Two thousand years and still it goes/To ponder his death and his life eternally.' I generally regard a chorus as a logical conclusion so, picking up my guitar, I sang the chorus which came to me spontaneously, put it on paper and said, 'Yes, there is a God and thanks be to God.'

I sang it to the girls who came to do the room, and sang it at least another dozen times during that same day, sometimes accompanied by Joe Thoma on fiddle. I could dissect aspects of the 'The Bright Blue Rose', and wax lyrical about its creation until the cows come home, but it happened exactly as I have described. It is a mysterious piece and nothing I could disclose would let you know any thing more about it, but I can honestly say, you will be glad when you sing it.

The Bright Blue Rose

I skimmed across black water
Without once submerging
On to the banks of an urban morning
That hungers first light much, much more
Than mountains ever do
And she, like a ghost beside me
Goes down with the ease of a dolphin
And awakens unlearned, unshamed, unharmed
For she is a perfect creature
Natural in every feature
And I am the geek with the alchemist's stone

Chorus *For all of you who must discover*
For all who seek to understand
For having left the paths of others
You find a very special hand

And it is a holy thing
And it is a precious time
And it is the only way
Forget-me-nots among the snow
It's always been and so it goes
To ponder his death and his life eternally

Chorus   *For all of you who must discover*
For all who seek to understand
For having left the paths of others
You find a very special hand

And it is a holy thing
And it is a precious time
And it is the only way
Forget-me-nots among the snow
It's always been and so it goes
To ponder his death and his life eternally
One bright blue rose outlives all those
Two thousand years and still it goes
To ponder his death and his life eternally

24

The Grip of Parallel

Almost a year on from our first visit, Claude and I returned to Ireland. We booked studio time in Ringsend's Ropewalk Studio and recorded the 'The Bright Blue Rose'. This pop, but good, version had only one airing when I sang it to its backing track on the RTÉ series *She's Got It* as Mary Black's guest. By now the accumulation of covers was very encouraging and the RTÉ television programme *Borderline* did a special called 'Jimmy MacCarthy, the Irish Songwriter'. Guests included Christy Moore who sang 'Ride On', Mary Black, with 'Katie', and Maura O'Connell, singing 'As I Leave Behind Néidín'. Mary Coughlan, sang 'Ancient Rain' and I closed the show with 'Adam At The Window'. Almost all were generous in their praise. It seemed the tide had turned.

Eleven years later there was another television tribute on Pat Kenny's 'Kenny Live' on RTÉ. I would like to take this opportunity to thank RTÉ Television for all their support over the years and to explain my one-man crusade last year (2001). I stated in newspaper interviews, while on a concert promotional tour of significant venues (the Nation Concert Hall Dublin, The Opera House Cork, The NEC Killarney, Christ Church Cathedral and Limerick University Concert Hall), that lack of airplay on RTÉ Radio was a great obstacle to the indigenous Irish music industry. This sector had a golden age with regard to airplay from the mid-1980s to the mid-1990s (which was humorously referred to as 'The Platinum Goose Years' by my astute friend, Noel Brazil), but from then on, support for it fell significantly. This is not an argument of the insular or the insolent. I know we must embrace the international repertoire, but not at the cost of our own national voice and indigenous recording industry, which is exactly what happened in New Zealand.

Recently I've noticed a great turn around in this. Long may it run. As a nation we would be much poorer without all RTÉ – both radio and television – has to offer.

After the recording of the *Borderline* tribute, Claude and myself went to see Danny Figis, ex-Virgin Prunes, perform with his multimedia show at the Irish Film Centre. He was accompanied by two dancers on platforms, one on either side of the stage. Claude left with one of these girls after the show, and I have not seen hide nor hair of him since then. He opened the way to better times for me, and proved himself a true friend. I think it's time to go and seek him out.

Flash back to my first month in Aarau, and to my encounter with the eccentric Swiss musician/producer, Martin Fischer, known as Chicken.

That first month, Chicken was production manager for an outdoor anti-nuclear concert, on the site of a plant at Gerskin, about 50 kilometres from Aarau. All of the acts involved got together to rehearse in an unused cinema. It was here that I met Anna, an anti-nuclear activist who, being part-Hopi Indian herself, spoke on the Rainbow Warrior prophecies of this North American tribe. It became blatantly obvious by the end of the first day that

133

she was on the verge of a nervous breakdown, but there is something unnervingly accurate about the perceptions of people in this wired condition. I wrote an anti-nuclear song for the day that was in it. It went along the lines of: 'In 1909, Tolstoy to Ghandi, what does it mean that thirty thousand weak and ordinary people have been able to subdue, two hundred million vigorous, clever, freedom-loving people. Now do not the figures make it clear, that it is not the English who have enslaved the Indians, but the Indians who have enslaved themselves, and it's the same today in a nuclear way', etc.

The day of the event arrived and I stood on a gigantic stage and watched a multitude of biblical proportions approach along three separate paths, also hundreds of riot police in full regalia.

The concert started and all was well. I chatted with Anna and she told me she knew the piper Davy Spillane and asked me if I would pass on to him a ring that she believed had magical properties. She told me to wear it myself until then and I agreed. It was a silver Venetian coin set in a gold Etruscan ring with the Doge and St Marco on one side and the Risen Saviour on the other. I was thirty-three years old and this was the grip of parallel.

I was next up to sing my new, anti-nuclear offering and I saw from the stage the beginnings of a scuffle, then smoke-trailing missiles flying through the air. The tear gas was unbearable, but I sang until I choked and could go on no longer. As the smoke screen lifted, I could see the crowd retreat in as orderly a fashion as they arrived. I could not help wondering what would have happened had this turn of events come about during my performances with Southpaw at the anti-nuclear concerts at Carnsore Point. The Swiss undoubtedly have a genius for method but a rebellious spirit just does not enter the equation.

The following morning, Chicken got a phone call to say that Anna had been committed to a mental hospital in Zürich. Shortly afterwards, I decided to travel to Venice by train and wrote the first half of 'The Grip Of Parallel' to the rhythm of the train and the remainder under the eye of the Lion.

The Grip of Parallel

One year to the day
Since I first met Magdalena
In the land of Helvetiae
On a freak and stormy day
She had a rival woman priestess
Of an ancient, red-skin people
And she gave me a coin of silver
Set in an Etruscan ring of gold
With the Doge and Saint Marco
And the risen Saviour facing forward
I was thirty-three years old
In the grip of parallel

Chorus *We were perfect in their footsteps*
We were dancers to the call
With the ring of a golden promise
On that beauteous first fall

135

So we followed it down to Venice
To where the lion smiled upon us
Saying here your guide was minted
The way is printed on your soul
And it's been worn since then
By the gaunt and thin
Who roam the roads of the
Inner landscape
They seek and seek the more
Into the grip of parallel

Chorus   *We were perfect in their footsteps*
We were dancers to the call
With the ring of a golden promise
On that beauteous first fall

Chorus   *We were perfect in their footsteps*
We were dancers to the call
With the ring of a golden promise
On that beauteous first fall

25

The Sky Road

The Dreamer's Lament · Love Divine

The Sky Road

Danny's made his mind up
He's leaving for America
He's leaving for America
Leaving us all behind
He says there's nothing here not drenched in beer
In blood and retribution
And the wealth distribution
Been weighing heavy on his mind
And he knows that he'll regret the leaving

Knows that he will pine for grieving
For the sky road by the singing sea
And all of us behind

Danny looks so lovely working in the fields
Or dancing like a wild one
Sparks flying around his heels
But his friends all gone before him
From the sacred ground that bore them
Where they wonder does she scorn them
For giving up the land
And they know that they'll regret the leaving
Know that they will pine for grieving
For the sky road by the singing sea
Alone and left behind

Danny's made his mind up
He's leaving for America
He's leaving for America
Leaving all of us behind
And I wonder does he know I love him
All below and none above him
As I sit here by the singing sea
Alone and left behind

The Dreamer's Lament

Oh Hannah I swear my heart you have broken
I'd wish for my death if light words are not said
And I'd give all I have for these words to be spoken
As I wait for the white-winged horse here on my bed
I remember the day of my heart and its hoping
When we walked on the sky road by that singing sea
When I first said I loved only you Hannah
And you said: 'Save no other, loved only me.'

Chorus *And the seals in the bay were engaged in their courting*
And the silver sky shone as if Heaven were near
But his mate went astray while his course he was holding
And from that day onwards he's been searching the sea

And I dreamed all last night and bad cess to my dreaming
I dreamed of the dark and depths of the sea
I dreamed in the fisherman's net she was tangled
And her true heart I again never would see

Chorus *And the seals in the bay were engaged in their courting*
And the silver sky shone as if Heaven were near
But his mate went astray while his course he was holding
And from that day onwards he's been searching the sea

During a visit to the West of Ireland, I stayed for a few days in Clifden – glorious Connemara, with its dramatic landscape and silvery light. It is easy to see why painters are drawn to this abundant source. It was a beautiful summer's afternoon when I headed out along the Sky Road from Clifden. Its naked and ghostly stone cottages, the trail of a jet in the clear blue of the sky above the abandoned homesteads all conspiring in a ready-made song of emigration.

I used the working title of 'The Connemara Song' for about five years while 'The Sky Road' lay sleeping among my countless collection of lyric scraps. Then, while working on my *Dreamer* album for Sony Records (1994) in Westland Studios, James Blennerhassett, wearing his musical director's hat for Frances Black, asked me if I had something suitable for her. I told him I had, but it was not quite there. Spending an hour in the piano booth, I completed the song. Then, ably assisted by the string arranger Fiachra Trench on piano, we recorded a mini-disc demo.

141

I must say that the version of 'The Sky Road' song, which is the title track on Frances Black's *Sky Road* album, is as good as any of the best recordings of my songs, and a personal favourite. It was produced by Arty McGlynn and featured the fiddle playing of Nollaig Casey, perfection itself.

'The Dreamer's Lament' was written during another trip to the West and was inspired by a local story of lovers who had passed that way. Travelling on the Sky Road, they came upon a púca, who put a spell upon them, changing them into seals. The fine turns of the story are long forgotten, nothing left but a song of love and loss. It's written to the air of 'Teddy O'Neill' and I could not resist this line from that song: 'I dreamed all last night, and bad cess to my dreaming'. But the thread of love divine stitched it all together, and yes, they did love again.

Love Divine

In your own good time
As we walk among the willows
As the leaves fall on our pillows
For love lost once more to find

And in your own good time
I believe a rose you'll send me
I believe this rose will mend me
With the thread of love divine

Chorus *Love divine*
Love divinely selected
For only the love
Ordained up above
And stitched by fire in his sight
With the thread of love divine

In your own good time
I won't be waiting for tomorrow
No longer burdened down by sorrow
With thoughts of clemency or crime

And in your own good time
I believe a rose you'll send me

I believe this rose will mend me
With the thread of love divine

Chorus *Love divine*
Love divinely selected
For only the love
Ordained up above
And stitched by fire in his sight
With the thread of love divine

26

What We Came Here For

The singer-songwriter Noel Brazil sadly passed away on 29 November 2001. He was a wonderful character, and will be sadly missed, but he left behind him a powerful body of work that any artist would be proud of. I have always thought of Noel as the Paddy Kavanagh of Irish songwriting and 'What We Came Here For' has echoes of McDaid's and The Catacombs, Kavanagh's watering holes, as portrayed by Anthony Cronin in his book *Dead as Doornails*.

Something of the same atmosphere surrounded our time in the Café Lorca in Cork, where we all hung out together in the early 1980s, whispering new ideas and drinking like there was no tomorrow. Noel was instantly recognised when he came to Cork, his spiritual home, by one of our chief name-givers Christy Twomey. Christy christened himself 'Handsome Drinking Chris Twomey', though others were not so fortunate: 'Scurvy Murphy', 'Black Dog' and 'Stab the Cat', are but a few of his inventions. But the name he bestowed on Noel was 'Vincie Venezuela', who was an exotic creature if ever we had known one.

What We Came Here For

You ask why we come here
And sit close together
Like birds of a feather
With no place to go
Singing songs of redemption
We'll be up 'till the dawning
With stories of what's yet to come and before
So we huddle together in the quest for the fire
And to quench the desire of what may be low
In the depths of our being
Where the light has no seeing
Where Christian and Jew lie reduced to mere gore

In the name of God
In the name of a country
In the name of sport
Of a King and his duty
In the name of love
In the name of war
And still you can ask me
What we came here for

What we came here for is a miracle
From where dream rivers flow
From where thoughts beyond space and time

Comes a glorious creature
Mute but a teacher
And will smile in her own, sweet time

You ask why we come here
Some buckled some dire
Pregnant with hope of celestial fire
In the depths of our being
That the light may know seeing
And you might not have to ask
What we came here for

27

The Pyramids at Sneem

James Scanlon, 'Scan' to his friends, is a Cork-based Kerry artist with a huge body of work, with an emphasis on stained glass. He has many kinds of public works, one being 'The Pyramids at Sneem'; cut stone structures with stained-glass inserts, standing at Sneem, County Kerry. I first met Scan with my brother Sean when they studied at the Crawford Art School, and though it seems like a hundred years ago, even then you could see their serious intent.

The Pyramids at Sneem

I know that you do love me,
But do wish that I was dead
Then to speculate the chasm's
Around my pale and muted head
In the grave with old O'Leary

And the horse behind half-door
And the ones who would devour their own
Call it culture
Making do with the want-to-bes
Who thrive upon the mores
Not appointed by my Heaven's Queen
But by conventions mere beaux gestes
See them graze around the midlands,
While the hungry scorch the hills
Where they reach to touch the Heavens
Where Heaven's pastures fill
But I'll throw my lot with Noel Brasil
And James Scanlon's stained-glass dreams
With those banished down to Sliabh Luachra
And the Pyramids at Sneem
I know that you do love me
Your ancient tattooed priest
How I rattle with your stones and bones
Each time I rise to speak
From the grave of old O'Leary
Where the horse danced caracóle
And the ones who would devour their own
Call it culture

28

No Frontiers

No Frontiers

If life is a river
Your heart is a boat
And just like a water-baby
Born to float
And if life is the wild wind
That blows way on high
Then your heart is Amelia
Dying to fly
Heaven knows no frontiers
And I've seen Heaven in your eyes
And if life is a bar room
In which we must wait

'Round the man with his fingers
On the ivory gates
Where we sing until dawn
Of our fears and our fates
And we stack all the dead men
In self-addressed crates
Heaven knows no frontiers
And I've seen Heaven in your eyes

In your eyes faint as the singing of a lark
That somehow this dark night
Feels warmer for the spark
Warmer for the spark
To hold us 'til the day
When fear will lose its grip
And Heaven has its way
Heaven knows no frontiers
And I've seen Heaven in your eyes

And if your life is a rough bed
Of brambles and nails
And your spirit's a slave
To man's whips and man's jails
And you thirst and you hunger
For justice and right
Then your heart is the pure flame
Of man's constant night

Heaven knows no frontiers
And I've seen Heaven in your eyes

In your eyes faint as the singing of a lark
That somehow this dark night
Feels warmer for the spark
Warmer for the spark
To hold us 'til the day
When fear will lose its grip
And Heaven has its way
And Heaven has its way
When all will harmonise
And know what's in our hearts
The dream will realise
Heaven knows no frontiers
And I've seen Heaven in your eyes

On reflection, I'm amazed that so much of my work came from my time in Switzerland. I must wander that way again. Walking through the French–Swiss border from St Louis into Basel, the stark contrast between the sleepy French checkpoint and the over-zealous Swiss begged me to profess that heaven knows no frontiers.

The first verse of this song clearly reflects my mother who, having been struck by the aviation bug at an early age, took to the skies and appeared in an article in the *Sunday Independent*, on 25 March 1962, as Cork's flying housewife. With the expected birth of twin brothers, Conor and Coleman, flying an Auster mono small craft became too much of a squeeze for safety and her wings were clipped just ten flying-hours short of her pilot's licence. My mother is a powerfully creative individual and can turn her hand to any art or craft; she passed on her passion for the visual arts to most of my siblings and the creative principle to us all. Most notable was her recognition and nurturing of my brother Sean's talent from an incredibly young age.

In the second verse, I can see my father, a colourful individual with a marked philosophical turn of phrase, standing by a piano, glass in hand, singing 'Red Sails In The Sunset'. The latter part of the verse is taken from his description of a life-after-death experience. He had suffered several massive coronaries within the same week. After the last, he was pronounced dead, but defied medical science and survived, giving us the gift of another twenty-six years of his unquenchable spirit. On recounting this experience to me in intensive care, he told me that he had felt absolute euphoria and, if it had not been for my five youngest siblings calling him back, he could have gladly gone to where we are all re-addressed to ourselves.

My father had a transport, accounts, and garage business at which he worked tirelessly to support his twelve children and, it must be said, in a style that was not common for the time. Not having been a great one for delegation, my father's absence through his illness soon brought the business into difficulty. My mother and I then decided to fold it down and sell his beloved Silvergrove, the house in which we had grown up.

Silvergrove was a cross between a holiday camp and a railway station. From the gate at the end of the avenue, you saw all of the trappings of opulence, a large garden, swimming pool and a string of cars parked in front

155

of a modern, American-style house. But it was a place of work, and we all worked. It was not unusual to have a sitting of twenty-five on any given day for meals. My parents, the twelve of us, three live-in help and a flow of drivers – characters of every hue lived here like one enormous family.

On putting Silvergrove on the market, we moved to Mount Pleasant, Bandon, County Cork, where we rented an old Georgian farmhouse. Here, the five youngest boys – twins Conor and Coleman, Desmond, and the very youngest, twins Mel and Felim – grew up as country boys. Out of hospital, and seeing this house for the first time, my shaken and depleted father stepped back and said, 'We'll all freeze here, Jim-Boy!'

This time was a real eye-opener for me, seeing who my parents really were. Though they had only meagre means at their disposal, through economy and ingenuity they maintained a quality of life that in some ways surpassed our previous existence. I think this is as good a time as any to say the thing that is rarely said – that my admiration for both my parents is boundless. They have guided and supported each and every one of us on our diverse paths right up to the present time.

29

The Morning of the Dreamer

Sacred Places

'The Morning Of The Dreamer' was given to me by an angel, while studying mindset techniques as envisaged through the ingenious concepts of Tony Quinn. Just like 'Sacred Places' it is the encapsulation, through the mapping of internal geography and creative visualisation, of my philosophy of art and spirituality. Anyone can engage in this high art, meditation and adventure. It's the artist's hand within your soul that creates the kingdom's sacred places, holy shrine, imagery eternal unto the soul divine. May the angel of the imagination be with you.

The Morning of the Dreamer

The last time that I saw him
He was lying in the sunshine
Saying, 'How are things in Heaven?'
To the birds up in the air
He said, 'All my rhyme and ramblings
Fall on deaf ears in this world
But it's all so clear indigo blue up there
And I'll come back in springtime
When the wind is blowing easy
When the pure light is shining in your hair
And we'll walk down Liberty Avenue
Right down Liberty Avenue
Right down Liberty Avenue.'

Chorus *Has anybody here seen the Dreamer?*
I left him here just yesterday
Ashes in the wind, waving to a friend
Living to believe he could wake the morning
The morning of the Dreamer
For the freedom of the slave
To be her own redeemer
And dare to leave the cave

In the emerald shallows
His arms will enfold you

Your dreams, your tears
Your love and bravery
And as we walk down Liberty Avenue
Right down Liberty Avenue
Right down Liberty Avenue
On the morning of the Dreamer
For the freedom of the slave
To be your own redeemer
And dare to leave the cave
And as a parting gift he gave me
These songs of glories that have been
A thousand more since Jesus Christ
As if we'll remember them

Chorus   *Has anybody here seen the Dreamer?*
I left him here just yesterday
Ashes in the wind, waving to a friend
Living to believe he could wake the morning
The morning of the Dreamer
For the freedom of the slave
To be your own redeemer
And dare to leave the cave

Sacred Places

To boldly go where none have gone before
Out on the seven seas
To tramp the windswept moors
Across the burning sand, the power of love to find
A choir of angels band unto the soul divine

And higher still to dance among the stars up in the sky
With the moon in your eyes and a clock on the wall
You will marry the two soon after you get the call
To go travelling beyond the dark
Follow the angels' song – it's just beyond the spark
All they're preparing for your dominion
They're blowing on the trumpets
And beating on the drum
It's the artist's hand within your soul
Creates the kingdom's
Sacred places, holy shrine
Imagery eternal unto the soul divine
Sacred places, holy shrine
Imagery eternal unto the soul divine

And in your darkest night, when devils stalk the land
The hand of love and light, where all might understand
Through where the angel of imagination ran
There you will learn of woman and of man

And higher still to dance among the stars up in the sky
With the moon in your eye and the clock on the wall
You will marry the two soon after you get the call
To go travelling beyond the dark
Follow the angels' song – it's just beyond the spark
All they're preparing for your dominion
They're blowing on the trumpets
And beating on the drum
It's the artist's hand within your soul
Creates the kingdom's
Sacred places, holy shrine
Imagery eternal unto the soul divine
Sacred places, holy shrine
Imagery eternal unto the soul divine

30

Strain of the Dance

November's Taboo

'The Strain Of The Dance' was originally recorded to be my first single but, out of respect to the victims of the Stardust tragedy and their families, Seamus O'Neill of Mulligan Records and I decided that the imagery that the song contained was best sidelined, and we agreed on a replacement, 'Miles Of Eyes'. On the B-side was 'Shuffle Of The Buckled', which was produced by Donal Lunny.

'The Strain Of The Dance' was my first cut as a songwriter, recorded by the musical force that was 'Moving Hearts' in the early 1980s. The singer at the time was Mick Hanley, himself a songwriter, whose work I love. It was performed at the Dominion Theatre in London, and recorded there for the album *Live at the Dominion*. As I read the credits on the album sleeve, it dawned on me for the first time that I had become a songwriter.

'November's Taboo' doesn't seem to fit in anywhere. It is the oldest of these fifty-three pieces and nobody seems to want it – but it keeps following me around. It is my black dog.

Strain Of The Dance

I'm walking to the corner now
I can't even hear a sound
My heart is beating way too fast
My feet can't even feel the ground
And I see you running too
A good thing that's what we found
And I see you running too
A good thing that's what we found

Chorus   *Under the night*
In the steel and the glass
Night city signs and the cars zipping past
The speed of the smile
And the quick, thieving glance
The dreams and the fears
And the strain of the dance

165

Rolling in the neon light
Feel hungry eyes that scan the night
Cold hands to a burning flame
Slows the quick and speeds the lame
And tears swell in the ancient eyes
Roll the reel to where they dry
And I see them running too
A good thing that's why they cry

Chorus   *Under the night*
In the steel and the glass
Night city signs and the cars zipping past
The speed of the smile
And the quick thieving glance
The dreams and the fears
And the strain of the dance
Strain of the dance

November's Taboo

In my heart's book
Things just don't look
Good for you at all
I dread the face of sheer disgrace
Behind it all
You'd think by now that I would know
The worth of such
To view the world through frozen eye
And still reserve the right to cry
Oh no, it's not me
Oh no, it's not I
It's November's taboo

In my mind's eye
A thunder sky surrounds it all
With demon eyes and peacock cries
It's Crazy Ball
You'd think by now that I would know
The worth of such
Here stuck inside a gambler's frame
And still can't even play the game
Oh no, it's not me
Oh no, it's not I
It's November's taboo

In my heart's book
Things just don't look
Good for you at all
This tower of strength
so far away
who'll walk around in bits
And say
Oh no, it's not me
Oh no, it's not I
It's November's taboo

31

The Parting

'The Parting' is a song about a boy leaving home for the first time to work as a man and return as one. He was a humorous and particularly cheerful character and, being sixteen years old or so, much the same age as I had been when I saddled-up Godolphin and left my hometown, I identified easily with him. (As an item of interest, Godolphin was one of three stallions in the evolution of today's thoroughbred racehorse. These three horses, the Byerley Turk, the Darley Arabian and the Godolphin Arabian are accepted as the three foundation sires of this breed.)

I would encounter Aodh O'Donnell, the boy in question, in the hall or in the kitchen and as he passed by he would thump his heart with his fist to the accompanying sound of Tha–Thump–Tha–Thump, communicating deep sadness.

All things nautical and sub-aquatic were Aodh O's great loves, I can still see him light up as he described to me three giant sea snails he had seen while scuba diving. His parents Jim and Mary O'Donnell were warm and hospitable people and I often experienced their generosity during my lean and more troubled years.

It seemed to be a natural and normal thing for this family to nurture and encourage talent and, since Aodh O' and his sister Eadín's maternal grandmother was the legendary Peggy Jordan, one might have thought it to be genetic.

In the course of this day, I casually picked up a copy of Kahlil Gibran's *The Prophet*, opening it at the heading 'Speak to Me of Children', which was the starting point for 'The Parting'.

The Parting

The parting brings its silence
Like the straining of a bow
No longer can he tarry
While his ship waits down below
Dips his fingers in the ocean
Leaves his old skin on the shore
One last loving look cast backwards
And the boy comes home no more

The solemn rock of the headland
And the singing stream rolls down
And my old wound reopened
When I left my own town
When I saddled Godolphin
Before I let the leathers down

171

One last loving look cast backward
In this dream of that boy's town

Chorus   *Aodh O' Aodh O' how quickly they go*
Diving for treasure below
Aodh O' Aodh O' how quickly they go
Diving for treasure
And leaving the care of them
Aodh O' Aodh O' how quickly they go
Diving for treasure below

The house already echoes to the sound of yesterday
To the wild and yielding wonder
Of some long lost child at play
Won't you stay 'till it be morrow
I heard the heartbeat call
One last loving look cast backward
Those last footsteps through the hall

Chorus   *Aodh O' Aodh O' how quickly they go*
Diving for treasure below
Aodh O' Aodh O' how quickly they go
Diving for treasure
And leaving the care of them
Aodh O' Aodh O' how quickly they go
Diving for treasure below
Aodh O' Aodh O' Aodh O'

32

On My Enchanted Sight

The Song of the Singing Horseman

On returning from my tour of America with DeDanann in 1986, I began my workout and swim routine again. One day, while sweating it out in the sauna, I got to chatting with Yod Murphy, brother of singer-songwriter Dave. Yod talked me into a working holiday at his Irish bar, The Man of Aran, in the Algarve. The sea and sunshine were a tonic and I even wrote the outline for a couple of songs. Some lines that were eventually used in 'The Morning Of The Dreamer' were written here. To be honest, the gigs themselves were used as an exercise in humility. I got into them and delivered to the best of my ability, but realised that I was not exactly what was required.

On returning to Ireland, I moved to Dublin, determined to record my first and long-awaited album. I approached Paddy Slattery of Slattery's, Capel Street, an established and well-known folk club venue and asked him for a Thursday night residence with the proviso of playing three weeks, then stopping for two; five weeks, stopping for one; eight weeks followed by another break, and so on. It was a huge success and though it was a small venue it was always chock-a-block.

It was during this time that I was introduced to Joe Fritsch and his wife Roxanne by Adele O'Dwyer, who I had met while working with DeDanann. Joe, an American who had a factory on the East Wall making care products for CDs and tapes, came to see me play in Slattery's accompanied by Adele on cello. I explained my predicament to this very capable man and he decided to set up a scenario within which an album could be recorded and possibly put out on our own label. Windmill Lane Studios were booked, but the recording master Brian Masterson, my first choice, was not available for the first leg of the work. Brian recommended the able, young John Grimes for this period.

175

In recording this album, we decided on a very pure approach; no electric instruments, no synthesisers, no click track. We wanted it to be organic in its essence. I produced it myself and felt confident that I was achieving what I had envisaged, having brought together the cream of Irish musicians – Steve Cooney, Nollaigh Casey, Davy Spillane, Paul McAteer, Adele O'Dwyer, Liam O'Maonlaí, Kevin Kenniff, Bill Whelan, James Blennerhasett, Lloyd Byrne, Mandy Murphy, Martín O'Connor and the brilliant Voice Squad. And I'm proud to have been the first to record the now celebrated choral group, Anúna.

Add all this top-flight talent to working in the best studio in the country and the budget becomes a terrifying reality.

Joe Fritsch, an astute businessman but one with little experience of the recording process, understandably decided to draw the line, fearing that I also lacked this experience. To the rescue came the wizard of sound recording,

Brian Masterson. He assured everyone that I had been doing a good job and continued the work with me to the end. The album finished, I decided to get a deal so that Joe and Roxanne could be paid, and this I achieved.

One day while in search of an album sleeve idea, I walked into the National Gallery. While walking through the Jack Yeats Room, I was struck by a picture in the distance and I thought to myself that if it had the right title it would be perfect. It had and it was. It was called *The Singing Horseman*. As I studied the image for a while – a boy sitting on a yellow horse singing to the blue sky – I thought it to be an Hallelujah. So I wrote one, 'The Song Of The Singing Horseman'.

I felt it would require an orchestra with an arrangement written by Bill Whelan; a choir, Anúna, with arrangement by Michael McGlynn; a stand-up band comprising Garvin Gallagher on double bass, Paul McAteer on drums, and Bill Whelan on piano; and the Voice Squad for good measure.

I was giving Cecil B De Mille a run for his money here. Now, how can I pay for this? My sincerest thanks to Billy Gaffe for helping me over this obstacle. With the advance given by the record company against the budget, I personally took the shortfall of £16,000. Having leased this album for ten years, over ten years and six months later, this financial equation remains the same.

A fair encapsulation of the whole affair might be that the very thing that makes you rich, makes you poor, but I would still prefer my wealth on the creative side of this ever-spinning coin.

My thanks to John O'Sullivan for his organisation and support in his role of executive producer of this project.

In 1991, the album was nominated for an RTÉ/AIB Art's award, it went to number two in the album charts, received excellent reviews without a shadow of criticism cast upon it.

The only songs from *The Song of the Singing Horseman* that I have not addressed are the title track itself and 'On My Enchanted Sight'. This was written under the shadow of Tadgh Mór MacCarthy's castle in Dripsey, County Cork, where I had wandered and elevated beauty to Goddess. Eleven is the number of tracks I've used on my album and when 'The Song Of The Singing Horseman' was added to this collection 'As I Leave Behind Néidín' was dropped. I was glad about this, as I felt it was too light in the company of the others.

On My Enchanted Sight

I was looking from my window
On the moon on a moonlit night
And everything was perfect
If not perfectly in sight
And it put my mind to wondering
Of the night we turned to day
Beneath the castle on Tadhg Mór's mountain
With our hearts being swept away
Hearts being a-swept, hearts being a-swept
Hearts being swept away

With the silver stream a-rushing
And a-pulling at our feet
And I'm glad I've known the hunger

177

And I'm glad I've seen it eat
I think I'll never see a beauty
Such as yours framed in that night
You wore it like a cloak, you did
On my enchanted sight
On my enchanted, my enchanted
My enchanted sight

My vision will not soar again
As was deemed on that fair night
When everything was perfect
If not perfectly in sight
How these souls that went a-wandering
On the liquid night did stray
Beneath the castle on Tadhg Mór's mountain
With their hearts being swept away
Hearts being a-swept, hearts being a-swept
Hearts being swept away

With the silver stream a-rushing
And a-pulling at their feet
When they sat down with the hunger
And the three of them did eat
I myself did paint this beauty
And did frame her in that night
This is the portrait of my love you see
On my enchanted sight

On my enchanted, my enchanted
My enchanted sight

With the release of this, my first album, I travelled more than ever, performing from Dingle to Donegal. Apart from the Everyman Theatre in Cork, the Olympia in Dublin was my first concert in my own right in a major venue. I was delighted to have had a full house, and a great review from Harry Browne in *The Irish Times* of 31 October 1991. The review ended: 'The rapport – with Jimmy MacCarthy momentarily pausing on his guitar before each chorus to invite the audience along – got a bit heavy at times, when not to know a lyric made one feel like one of the damned in a choir full of the elect. But it was a fine evening's entertainment.'

By the spring of 1993, I was badly in need of rest and a holiday in sunshine so, to begin with, I went to New York to visit John O'Mahony, who had by now moved from Harlem. Then on to Nashville where I was taken care of so well by my kind friend, the darling girl from Clare, Maura O'Connell and her husband Mac Bennett. Maura, who works with the legendary dobro player/producer Jerry Douglas, has recorded many of my songs since the beginning of my writing career, but her version of 'Love Divine' with my great hero James Taylor is to die for. One other song that I must mention here, is her recording of 'Mystic Lipstick' *as Gaeilge*, and it is not so much a translation as altogether another vision. The Irish title was 'Aisling Gear' and it is perfectly written by the poet Liam O'Muirthile.

Maura introduced me to all the folk on Nashville's Music Row and, as a result of this, I was to return and write with the Nashville writers – Pat Alger, Craig Bickheart and, most especially, Kent Robbins, who has since sadly passed away. Kent, a serious man, was not the most typical of Nashville writers. He had the reserve of a high court judge, spoke with some authority on William Blake and I liked him very much. We wrote, what I still feel is a great song, 'A Dance As Old As Tears'. This song has been well performed by Sean Keane, and produced by the legendary producer Jim Rooney, but I still think it could fly much higher.

Scott Gunter, who works for Almo Irving Music, Nashville, was responsible for setting up all of these co-writes. (Hey Scott, when are you going to get me a cut out there?)

My next stop was California, to visit my old friend from our days with the Dixie Showband, bass player Mick Cunningham and, as they used to say when we arrived to play anywhere, 'Look at them, not a Dixie among them!' Mick met me at Los Angeles airport, we drove to Santa Barbara and, to use California-speak, the place was a trip. Mick and his wife Delia lived on an avocado ranch, a veritable paradise where explosions of life and colour abounded. Mick had two horses and a pet mule, Ena, a bizarre-looking creature, strawberry roan, standing about 15.3.

We went out riding most days and, on one happy trail in particular, we rode through Rose Valley along the Sespi River. That day reunited me with God through the prayer of all that is of itself. Nature in all its magnificence. There is something about riding in sunshine through beautiful country that is a balm for the spirit and this day most certainly was. Back in the pick-up and on our way home, the scent of orange groves permeated everything as we listened in silence to Van Morrison's glorious 'Avalon Sunset'. This was a special time and is still a treasured memory.

The Song of the Singing Horseman

I find complete peace of mind
From this friend who comes to woo me
What a faithful mount
Never faltered, never threw me
Leaped from pages of the Book of Light
Wordless through eternity, illuminating all
Its light will seek the equalising energy
It's the blue light of His Holy Cross
It's the white winged horse
It's the song of the singing horseman
For every burdened heart and his own

Chorus   *I want you, I want you in my life my Lord*
The child within my heart and on my word my Lord
I'd love you, I'd love you in my life my Lord
The child within my heart, and on my word my Lord

This is a prayer boat
So that it may float on down
To the feet of the Lord
Burning bright above confusion
Rising up with the Hallelujah
Glory Glory Hallelujah
Begone unholy winds
From Hallowed Halls call godly friends

It's the blue light of His Holy Cross
It's the white winged horse
It's the song of the singing horseman
For every burdened heart and his own

Chorus *I want you, I want you in my life my Lord*
The child within my heart and on my word my Lord
I'd love you, I'd love you in my life my Lord
The child within my heart, and on my word my Law

33

The Carrier of Scandal

The Carrier of Scandal

He's a storyteller and a keyhole dweller
And a carrier of scandal
The first to come and the last to go
He's a dirt bird, a vulture and a scald crow

So keep one eye open wherever you go
For the carrier of scandal
And his travelling show
Keep your heart in your pocket
And a lock on your tongue
For the carrier of scandal

He ridicules your estranged friend
And he'll be your bosom buddy
As the story goes, see the vulture gloat
And you're picked to the bones of your body
So keep one eye open, wherever you go
For the carrier of scandal
And his travelling show
Keep your heart in your pocket
And a lock on your tongue
For the carrier of scandal

To Mister-must-know and Mister-must-tell
Keep an eye on the mirror when you trip on the bell
For the wages of gossip is relentless hell
And a sentence of mute solitary
And there's no one to talk to and no one to tell
For the carrier of scandal when he trips on the bell
Keep your heart in your pocket
And a lock on your tongue
For the carrier of scandal
For the carrier of scandal

'The Carrier Of Scandal' is the oldest of the songs from my *Dreamer* album. I had been told a story about a friend of mine and his activities during a particular evening in Thomastown, near Kilkenny. I listened without speaking to this scandal, realising that, on the evening in question, I had been in the company of the person whose behaviour was being censured, so, knowing that nothing of the kind had taken place, I berated the scandal giver.

My thanks to Christy Moore for allowing me to use a line from his song 'Scaldcrows' for my printed version in this book.

I guess journalism is like anything else, good and bad, but too often the balance between the two is scary. From my numerous interviews and promotional articles, which are crucial to any performing artist, I can remember only a handful of journalists quoting me verbatim. I do not refer to this as inferior journalism per se, as it is obviously a very fallible art. Though I am truly grateful for the promotion and completely understand the fallibility, I would like to set the record straight with regard to a few of these inaccuracies, trivial and all as these points may seem. Firstly, my father never had a soul music collection; he just wouldn't have been a Smokey Robinson fan. Secondly, my grandfather was not a horse trainer. I will not go on but the extended family knows about these things and no one needs their word put in question.

All of this took place at Mornington Crescent Tube station in Camden Town, London, and, on that same day, I had noticed Elton John, who turned out to be the innocent, being torn limb from limb on the front page of *The Sun* newspaper. I went home and wrote this scathing, Brechtian theatrical piece about this generic human weakness and yellow journalism. The song was written on a Wurlitzer piano while watching the movie *Cabaret* on an old black-and-white television with the sound turned down.

34

The Highest Point

The Perfect Present

'The Highest Point' is a song about aspiring to reach the summit – to have a dream. My particular dream is to write a truly great song – but it can relate to a dream of any kind, for anyone.

'The Perfect Present' is written about living in the now. In life, we generally spend most of our time lamenting what has happened, dreading what might happen and consequently losing the only thing we've got – this moment, the perfect present.

The Highest Point

I was dreaming of my love
With her hair tied up above
That fair face that lights my soul
She must have stolen it from an angel
We were dancing by the sea
Said how she'd been missing me
And the sweetness of a song set free
A song sung over and over and over
Nights in dreams of Heaven blue
Stitched and fused as one we flew
'Til I awoke again and knew
That my heart is always waiting

Chorus *Still I wonder why I follow her*
And I wonder why I care
As I lift my face up from my hands
Again I find her there
She's the dread of my nightmare
She's the love of my life
You see, a dream can be the highest point
We reach within a life
And I wonder why I care

On the breeze, the spirit muse
She calls me out and leaves me clues

She sings sean-nós and she sings the blues
And her fool again pushed over
We were dancing by the sea
Said how she'd been missing me
And the sweetness of a song set free
A song sung over and over and over

Chorus *Still I wonder why I follow her*
And I wonder why I care
As I lift my face up from my hands
Again I find her there
She's the dread of my nightmare
She's the love of my life
You see, a dream can be the highest point
We reach within a life

Within a life
A dream can be
The highest point
Within a life
A dream can be

The Perfect Present

Where is the gift that you promised to me?
I've been searching forever – now where can it be?
It's not in the hallway that letter I see
Someone's 'I love you' more than I love me
It's not in the mountains or under the sea
The sun and moon above me
The stars that shine on me

Though walking through holly and halls
Glistening gold
I am walking in slavery, just won't be told
That here is the moment, this moment alone
The dream realised; the heart will be flown
Over the mountains and under the sea

Chorus   For it is in the perfect present
If only you would see
Love yourself, know the moment
What wonders then can be?
In the perfect present
Glory, glory be
Love yourself, know the moment
What wonders then can be?

Where is the gift that you promised me?
Where is the love that will set my soul free?
When will my fame and good fortune untold?
Will the magic of alchemy do as you've told?
Where is the gift that you promised to me?

Chorus   For it is in the perfect present
If only you would see
Love yourself, know the moment
What wonders then can be?
In the perfect present
Glory, glory be
Love yourself, know the moment
What wonders then can be?

35

Lorraine · Shadowy

The *Dreamer* album itself may not have achieved all that I hoped for, but, at the time, I had developed chronic asthma and, not being in anything like the best of shape, the proceedings were impeded and the potential of a splendid offering lost. What saddened me most about this was how badly I had served some of my best songs, but it does have its own particular charm and has a very soothing effect, particularly because of the filmic and beautiful string arrangements by Fiachra Trench.

Two songs from it are 'Lorraine', a contemporary, surreal and urban ballad, and 'Shadowy', a song I love, which is the ancient tale of doomed lovers.

Lorraine

She was a beauty
She was a belle
She was something to behold
So gather 'round me
And listen well
For this story must be told
Hand-in-hand across the sky
Hounds snapping at their heels
Love of loves and how it feels
She was the shadowy
And he was the steal
She was all womankind
And he was learning to kneel
At the foot of the mountain
At the roots of mankind
At the breath of this frozen child
Lost in space and time

Chorus *Where are you now, my sweet love?*
Where are you now, my pain?
Where are you now, my sweet love?
Where are you now, my love Lorraine?

She had a husband
A man as any man

But she saw him as an Arab dancing on
The desert floor
But he could not understand
This web of fantasy
So she danced for him no more
She came down from the sky
But lost her mind on high
Love of loves and how it feels
She was the shadowy
And he was the steal
She was all womankind
And he was learning to kneel
At the foot of the mountain
At the roots of mankind
At the breath of this frozen child
Lost in space and time

Chorus   *Where are you now, my sweet love?*
Where are you now, my pain?
Where are you now, my sweet love?
Where are you now, my love Lorraine?

I found her and I lost her
I may never rest again
If I can't make that woman she
My lover and my friend

Shadowy

I built you an altar with the God of happiness
A Buddha, a glass dolphin and a brooch
By The Potato Diggers and the Goose Girl beside them
Golden earrings that caused such reproach

And a Christmas novena of Joseph and Mary
Under palms on a bridge of a brook
And I did love you, placed none above you
You stole me away, Shadowy
You stole me away, Shadowy

Chorus *Oh, oh, oh, Shadowy*
Oh, oh, oh, Shadowy

She may be in Durban or in Ballyhaunis
While the dragon is hiding the moon
And I'd love to forgive her and I long to be with her
Still in vain search and search for the tune

And I oft think I see her on the pier by the seashore
Or on the hill where we made heather beds
And I did love you, placed none above you
You stole me away, Shadowy
You stole me away, Shadowy

Chorus   *Oh, oh, oh, Shadowy*
            Oh, oh, oh, Shadowy

Soon after *Dreamer* came out, I was approached to be one of four in a package that was to be known as Four for the Road. This was the brainchild of Barry Gaster of the Gasworks Agency. We toured the country twice and released an album under the same name with Sony Records. The others in the line-up were Mick Hanley, Finbar Furey and Don Baker. It was a successful project, but fell very far short of its sister predecessor *A Woman's Heart*, which, I think, Barry had modelled this venture on. God loves a trier. Well done!

36

The Music of Love · Original Doubt

Love Don't Fail Me

The Music of Love

Love is the answer, whatever the question
And the harvest of love can be easily grown
You reap what you sow, so they tell me
I've been walking through this field of dreams
Just to find my way home

Everybody's looking for that special someone
Someone to make them feel more than they feel

When they are alone
Stop looking out for what's already within you
And you won't have to worry
And you won't have to roam
I'm talking about a higher love
I'm talking about a love above
Anything I've ever known

Chorus   *Can you feel it in the moonlight*
Can you feel it in the daylight
All the magic of your life
It's the music of love
You know it doesn't have a season
You know it doesn't need a reason
And to miss it would be treason
It's the music of love

You say you are lost and you are brokenhearted
You say the world won't do what you want the world to do
You're all decked out and just can't wait to get started
But somehow you keep on missing the queue
Love is the answer whatever the question
And the harvest of love can be easily grown
You reap what you sow, so they tell me
Keep on walking through that field of dreams
Till you find your own
I'm talking about a higher love

I'm talking about a love above
Anything I've ever known

Chorus   *Can you feel it in the moonlight?*
Can you feel it in the daylight?
All the magic of your life
It's the music of love
You know it doesn't have a season
You know it doesn't have a reason
And to miss it would be treason
It's the music of love

Original Doubt

The scene is set in an open space
He stands accused in his Father's place
He was dressed in black, in original doubt
The court was mute, he was screaming out
I need sacred sanctuary; inner-hallowed ground
No mere magistrate can tell me where is lost and what is found

Blood upon the open page
Armed with nothing but a singer's rage
And the court adjourned to an archaeological
Dig manned by a solitary guinea pig

Chorus Seeking sacred sanctuary
Inner-hallowed ground
No mere magistrate can tell me
Where is lost and what is found

Bridge Book of life, wordless through eternity, unchain my heart
Book of life, equalising energy, unchain my heart

The verdict's in and the victim cast
Forgive me Father for your own past
I was dressed in black
In original doubt
The court was mute, I was screaming out

Chorus   *I need sacred sanctuary*
Inner-hallowed ground
No mere magistrate can tell me
Where is lost and what is found

Bridge   *Book of life, wordless through eternity, unchain my heart*
Book of life, equalising energy, unchain my heart

Love Don't Fail Me

I've been lost and lonely
Searching for the one and only
I might as well be walking on the moon
Looking in at other lives
With envy that I can't disguise
I was feeling like a guitar out of tune
Then in flew the sunshine and out ran the rain
And trumpets from Heaven
Blow sweetly for me once again

Chorus *O love don't fail me now*
O love don't fail me now
January hold together
Soon will be more clement weather
O love don't fail me now

And even though the snows are falling
The hopeful time of summer's calling
City streets just can't seem to tell
Under neon lights the eyes are thieving
With the empty hearts of the disbelieving
But I will be a light unto my self
I'll glow with the life light; I'll dance with the rain
And trumpets from Heaven
Blow sweetly for me once again

Chorus   *O love don't fail me now*
               O love don't fail me now
               January hold together
               Soon will be more clement weather
               O love don't fail me now

Heading into the second year here in Wicklow in the late 1990s, living and working had developed its own rhythm. My musical existence had by now almost totally left my consciousness, and I played like a boy at being involved in the world of horses. I took to buying young animals for small money, and would ride them around the roads and headlands high above Rathnew and Wicklow; I was truly in my heaven.

This phase began when I bought a small thoroughbred mare from the kingly Tommy O'Brien. Over a period of time, I bought another five horses from him and all were exactly as he had said they would be. One of these, a three-quarter bred grey gelding by Nearly A Nose, has gone on to become quite a successful eventer. Later, I was to hear Tommy referred to as the 'King of the Travellers' and was not in the least surprised.

The first horse I bought from him, I named Lucky. She was only partially broken and had no mouth but, within a few weeks, I discovered she could turn on a sixpence and thought she might make a polo pony. I phoned a good friend, Ruth Elliott, who managed a polo yard for Mickey Herbst near Brittas Bay. Within a week or two Raffael Le Desma, an Argentinean maker of polo ponies, came to see me and bought Lucky for the Herbst yard. Having put her through her paces, he thought her capable of the job and rode her in competition successfully.

A year or so later, Raffa approached me to know where we could get twenty or so animals like Lucky. What immediately sprung to my mind were the rejected animals from the Curragh; small, failed racehorses who are sold to the knacker's yard for the price of their meat. I contacted some horse dealers around Kildare who trafficked in these horses, and Raffa and I headed off early one morning over the Wicklow Mountains to Newbridge. We arrived at an old, unused farmyard that led out onto a large meadow where there must have been fifty or so horses. A few were injured, but most were perfect and beautiful creatures.

We brought them into a large barn, separating and releasing them as we went. Those familiar with horses will know the electricity, the visual dynamics and the almost alarming energy levels that surround this type of procedure. Raffa cast an expert's eye over the animals for the required points of conformation and we decided on the most suitable twenty-three animals to be delivered to my yard the following day.

Unfortunately, the deal on the selling of these horses fell through and they were now grazing in the paddock behind the yard. I had no idea what to do with them but I had one contact number in the polo world in England, QC Brady. I spoke to him and he came to see the horses himself. This tall, handsome and fit-looking seventy year old with a shock of white hair, appeared to me more like an angel than the gentleman he obviously was. He returned with his driver a week later in the early hours of the morning, slept for an hour, had a coffee, loaded the horses and returned home again. As I watched the tail-lights of the lorry disappear into the distance, my joy was threefold;

207

I had had a great adventure, a fair profit, and the good karma of having saved these beautiful animals from a cruel fate.

Around this time, I had been involved in a few fundraisers for Loughlinstown Hospital – concerts at St Columcille's Church – which were very successful and enjoyable. The first of these made no indentation on the security my new existence had given me but, driving home a year later after the second concert, I felt drunk with the music and the need to perform again.

Shortly after this, I was contacted by Jim McAllister of Comhaltas Ceoltóirí Éireann to headline the first Clasach Concert at the National Concert Hall. The guests of honour were the President of Ireland, Mary McAleese and her husband Dr Martin McAleese. Two days later I received a letter from the president that moved me deeply. I have met many famous people, but very few with such warmth and generosity

208

One thing led to another and Pat Egan agreed to take me on in a manager/promoter capacity. To my amazement, we were selling out significant concert venues and smaller art centres around the country. All of this was very encouraging, especially with not having had a record out for five years. Then a dream came true. From 24–26 October 1999, I was asked to perform with Sir George Martin, the fifth Beatle, at the National Concert Hall. The line-up of singers was Eimer Quinn, Lesley Dowdall, Brian Kennedy, Sean Keane, Liam O'Maonlaí and myself, and we were accompanied by a seventy-piece orchestra, a stand-up band, backing singers and conducted by this kind and charming gentleman. To love The Beatles as I did and to experience this brief but magical mystery tour with the most successful producer/arranger in popular music history is one of my most cherished musical memories.

Around this time, I approached Joe O'Reilly of Dara Records with the compilation idea for *Warmer for the Spark*, a collection of my most successful songs by the artists who had brought them to prominence. Like water flowing down a hill, it was an effortless success. This opened up new possibilities as the legendary Louis Walsh suggested that I should send a copy of this album to the major publishing companies. Eventually I was signed by Mike McCormack to Universal Music Publishing with a sizeable advance that, in my mind, came under the banner BUILD YOUR OWN STUDIO NOW, which I did.

The Universal deal introduced me to co-writing with English pop writers, such as Tim Laws, who has written for Gabrielle and The Lighthouse Family, and Graham Lyle, who wrote 'What's Love Got To Do With It' for Tina Turner and too many other great pop songs to list here. I could never have guessed what a blast it would be to work with people who are so good at what they do, among them Tom Nicholls, Shepard Solomon, Wayne Hector, Steve Mac, Russ Ballard, Gary Burr and the stunningly brilliant Conor Reeves.

209

Shortly before the Universal signing came about, The Corrs recorded 'No Frontiers' for their unplugged album, the sales for which were colossal. This was a major factor in me being signed. My thanks and sincerest best wishes to all of them, not forgetting their gifted guitarist Anto Drennan.

I am continuing to perform concert venues all around the country but now I am accompanied by two great singers, Mandy Murphy and Lynn Kavanagh. Singing with them is like flying to heaven on Concorde and never fails to lift my heart. With Pat Egan as my manager I had, for the first time, truly professional representation, a commodity that is in very short supply in the Irish music business. Pat's work as a promoter was also impeccable.

During 1999–2000, I needed something new to keep me alive, so I set up my own record label, Ride On Records. First, I put out my own version of 'The Contender' and later 'The People Of West Cork And Kerry'. On this label, I also released The Celtic Tenors' first single, my song 'Mystic Lipstick', which I arranged and produced for them.

With my new studio now built and a trial-run recording of 'The People Of West Cork And Kerry' completed, my co-producer Pat O'Donnell and I set to work on my next album. I chose Pat because I admired his work on the Kieran Goss album *Worse than Pride*, but his electric and acoustic guitar playing was a bonus I was not expecting. We worked for a year on *The Moment*, which is a much more contemporary production than my previous offerings, and five of the eleven tracks are co-writes with some of the luminaries mentioned earlier.

During this time, my nephew Christopher Wall, who was fifteen at the time, came for two weeks' work experience in the studio and to perform as my guest at Christ Church Cathedral. I asked him on arrival if he had started writing songs yet, he answered 'bits and pieces', which he then played for me. One figure that he played struck me instantly and we spent the next day completing the structure, which I immediately wrote a lyric for and titled 'The Music Of Love'.

Christopher plays piano on 'Music Of Love' and he also recorded my vocal and acoustic guitars. He is a multi-talented individual who plays several instruments, including the piano, brilliantly, and is a really good singer. He must take after my brother Ted who has a sweet singing voice. I hope that fortune shines on me so that I may work with Christopher again, but I suspect that he will be swept away to a higher place, and this would please me even more.

July 5th 2002 was the release date of my next album, *The Moment*, and the first single is 'The Music Of Love'. *The Moment* goes out on Ride On Records through Cog Communications, also available from the website www.jimmymaccarthy.com. This is to be followed by *The Collected Jimmy MacCarthy* in late autumn 2002. I can hardly believe I'm hearing myself saying all of this, but I am my only realistic option. So be it!

On St Patrick's weekend 2001, I was performing at the National Concert Hall; it was a great night on all fronts, brilliant sound by the unsurpassable Mark Kennedy, a wonderful audience and I was able to say 'I told you so' to someone who had lost all belief in my future as a performer.

The following day, I phoned a friend of mine, the actor Patrick Bergin, to tell him I had seen him in the TV movie *Patrick*. He replied, 'And I saw *you* at the Concert Hall.' Sometime before, I had run the idea of staging a musical re-telling of the Jack Doyle Story past Patrick, but the penny had dropped for him during my introduction to 'The Contender' that night in the Concert Hall.

I had originally written 'The Contender' after reading a wonderful film script about Jack Doyle by the writer Michael Sheridan. This project had gone sideways, but never say never. We – Michael, Patrick and me – decided to meet up the following week to commit ourselves to telling the greatest Irish story never told.

211

Over the next few weeks, we spoke by telephone and the ensuing flood of ideas began to form an outline. I documented most of these ideas and these notes later became invaluable. I realised at this point that, to bring all of this together, we would need someone with skills beyond our own. I had been a director on the board of the Irish Music Rights Organisation (IMRO) since its inception and had witnessed the organisation being brought to independence, becoming a model of its kind and improving the lot of Irish composers and publishers a hundred-fold, under the baton of Hugh Duffy. I contacted the now-retired Hugh and asked if he would help us form a company to get things moving. He agreed and we formed Contender Productions.

By 2002, we have written a sixteen-scene treatment and recorded a CD of ten songs with a narration by Patrick. We have performances by Sinead

O'Connor as Movita, Matthew Gilsenan, of The Celtic Tenors, as young Jack Doyle, Patrick Bergin as the older Jack and Mary Coughlan as Dolly Fawcett, the Bordello keeper. We have Anúna as well and much more. There remain three or four song to be completed, a little nip and tuck, then, next year, we send *The Contender* stage musical out into the world – to court the great producers, successfully, we hope.

Let me now address 'Original Doubt' a deep concept addressing trans-generational issues. It is a song of healing and of letting go of the futility of blame. 'The Song Of The Singing Horseman' and 'Wonder Child' owe a part of their formation to the bridge section of this song.

'Love Don't Fail Me' is a song of hope in the aftermath of love lost. I should say, at this point, that in most of my songs, you will find a common philosophical thread, with lines or partial lines reused to reinforce a personal philosophy. Take, for instance, the first line from 'The Music Of Love': 'Love is the answer whatever the question.' This line comes from a song, 'Angels' Wings', that I wrote many years ago. Then, during one of my first co-writes for Universal with Wayne Hector and Steve Mac, I introduced this chorus as the starting point for the song that would then be 'Angels' Wings' – version 2. New supporting verses were written, and it was released on the Westlife No. 1 album *Coast to Coast*.

37

Still In Love

Still In Love

And the bells played an Angelus
And the whole world stood still
As I walked out on main street
Leaving all that might have been
And I cursed the silver needle
As I cursed the powers that be
And I curse the bloody bigotry
That has stolen the sacred key
I am still in love
I am still in love
I am still in love
So very much in love

And the bells played for Gandhi
And for Martin Luther King
And a thousand more since Jesus Christ
As if we'll remember them
And the bells played an Angelus
And the whole world stood still
She was wrapped up snug on Main Street
Melting Armageddon's chill
I am still in love
I am still in love
I am still in love
So very much in love

'Still In Love' has been with me a long time. It was written when everyone was talking about the Nostradamus predictions, and I was greatly interested in the man who saw through time. One day, on St Patrick's Street in Cork, I met a friend with her little girl who was wrapped up snug in her buggy. While I was rambling on about Nostradamus this little one flashed a smile at me and Armageddon was no more – I am still in love.

Divine Love now dissolves and dissipates
Every wrong condition in my mind, body and affairs
Divine Love is the strongest chemical in the universe
And dissolves everything which is not of itself

Ride on
See ya

Permission Notice

The cover quotation from *One Voice – My Life in Song* by Christy Moore is reproduced by permission of Hodder & Stoughton Limited.

OF SCANDAL', 'HARLEM', 'WONDER CHILD', 'THE MORNING OF
THE DREAMER' and 'SACRED PLACES': words and music by Jimmy
MacCarthy. By kind permission of Sony Music Publishing.